How To Write Faster

Strategies for Planners and Pantsers

Acknowledgements

I'd like to thank those who took the "Strategies of a Fast Writer" surveys, gave feedback on the evolving manuscript, and helped me brainstorm the strategies. The workshops generated a wealth of ideas and insights, which I then stole and put into the book. The Pantser planning section in particular would not exist without their contributions.

Chris Alderman, Brian Baker, Mike Bresner, Lynn Cooper, Susan Diranian, John Dwight, Angela Felsted, Mary Ellen Gavin, Marian Gravel *née* Hayes, Stephanie Groot, Farida Haque, Caroline Hayes, Marlene Hayes Dorneich, Rachel Hayes Fast, Eleanor Huteson, Jeffrey Jacobs, Jenn Johnson, Jessica Jones, Laura Jones, David Keener, Bill Krieger, Lou Lamoureaux, Jennifer Loizeaux, James Marconi, Marissa, Joanne McAlpine, Gordon McFarland, Jerry Moore, Jeff Patterson, Michael Reiland, Donna Royston, Brigitta Rubin, Alana Rudkovsky, Steve Skeetz., Beth Sadler, Heidi Schandler, Adam Shannon, Stephanie Siebert , and Mark Zimmermann

With special thanks to John R. Hayes for developmental editing and to Karen Schriver for document design advice for this book.

Snail clipart by Brad Fitzpatrick Illustration
www.bradfitzpatric.com

i

To John R. Hayes

The most famous writing researcher in the world,
and an even greater dad.

Contents

Introduction

"Successful writing comes through effort similar to that of a farmer. No magician's wand, but rather a rake, a bandanna for sweat, and a sunup to sundown work ethic."

Catherine Haar,
writing researcher

Why Did My Writing Slow Down?

I picked up a pen for the first time three years ago. I've always had stories in my head, but until then, I'd never written them down. Then, when there was a serious illness in the family, stories began swirling around in my head until I couldn't concentrate. *If I can get just them down on paper, maybe they'll give me some peace.* Wrong. Writing them down just encouraged them.

I wrote quickly at first. My initial effort, a short novel, took three weeks to complete. A beginner's effort, it was written in narrative exposition, using omniscient voice with lots of head-hopping.[1] As a new writer, I was able to produce 2000 words a day, mainly because I had no idea what I was doing.

Little by little, I learned the craft of writing. My sister, who'd taken a class in creative writing, said they'd been taught to Show not Tell. I didn't know what that meant. My friend Heidi told me about POV. I didn't know what that meant, either, so I got myself some "How to Write" books and found out.

---

[1] Narrative exposition, or 'tell', is the easiest style in which to write. It tells what happened without going into detail. In omniscient voice, the thoughts of all characters are known, as well as past and future events. Head-hoping means switching from one point-of-view character to another rapidly, sometimes within the same paragraph.

I wrote a second story using my new skills. It took longer to write than the first, even though it was shorter.

In the fall, when I'd been writing for about a year and a half, I joined a writers' group and the quality of my writing doubled almost overnight. Narrative exposition was replaced by Show not Tell, omniscient POV gave way to third person limited. I was told that my characters moved through empty space, so I learned to build descriptions full of motion and symbolism.

At Thanksgiving, while the cousins chased the cat around the house with what looked like a yarn octopus suspended from the end of a fishing pole, I sat on the sofa with a pad of paper, trying to describe a rider crossing an old lava flow that blocked the road.

I could see it clearly, the reins in the man's hand, the horse's reluctance to leave the road, the yellow flowers springing up from folds in the grey rock. I'd been to Hawaii where I'd seen wildflowers growing in recently hardened lava, but I couldn't translate it into words.

After I'd scribbled and crossed out for over an hour, my dad came over and asked me what I was working on so intensely. I had little to show, my finished text amounted to only a few inches of longhand on the page. My word count had dropped from 2000 words a day to something like 220, or two thirds of a page a day.

And then I discovered Deep POV, which slowed me down even more. Unlike third person limited, where the reader sits on the character's shoulder, in Deep POV, the reader *is* the character. Deep POV grabs the reader's emotions at a visceral level and is widely used in romance and horror. [2]

Deep POV made a huge difference in my writing. I started getting more fan mail than before, and it said things like, "By the last scene I was sobbing" or "Even though I knew how it would end, I was biting my nails from suspense." Deep POV is harder to write than third person limited, and it takes longer, but the emotional impact it gave to

---

[2] The invention of Deep POV is attributed to Stephen King.

writing was worth it. However, it came at a cost. My writing speed dropped to 170 words a day, about half a page a day of polished text.

I couldn't afford to write slowly. I had only so much writing time, in the quiet half hour before the kids came downstairs in the morning, on the back of an envelope waiting for a school play to start, or in the five minutes before the spaghetti water boiled over.

Panicked about my plummeting word count, I began to read books about how to write faster. It was then that I first encountered PDR in Jeff Bollow's excellent book, *"Writing Fast: How to write anything with lightning speed"*.

PDR stands for Plan, Draft, Revise. It's a writing strategy in which you plan what you're going to write, sketch out a rough draft as quickly as possible, and revise your draft first for plot structure, then for wording. Copy editing is not one of the tasks of PDR, and should be postponed until after the manuscript is completely finished.

The brilliant thing Bollow did was take the PDR model, originally developed to teach students how to write like expert writers, and use it to help already expert writers write faster.

Most novice writers don't plan or revise at all, but experienced writers sometimes revise in the wrong order. The structured PDR approach can help limit excessive revision. I started using it, and right away, my word count went from 170 to over 300 words of finished writing a day. *Where have you been all my life?*

There was only one problem. The PDR books were written by Planners, for Planners. I had a foot in each camp, in that major parts of my stories revealed themselves while I was writing, long after the outline stage.

The Causes of Slow Writing

There are several things that slow your writing down. Skilled writing takes time, just like any other skilled craftsmanship. And no one is 100% efficient, it's normal to throw out larger scraps than one would like or redo something that's already been done.

It's also possible to believe you're writing slowly, when you're completely normal, but measuring yourself by the wrong standard.

1. Skilled Writing Takes Time

The fact is, skilled writing takes time. Anne Becker, a writing researcher at Oakland University in Michigan, observed that novices tend to write in narrative exposition, the fastest of all writing styles. "Narrative takes the least amount of effort, possibly because writers at every ability have practiced this genre since they started to write. [3]"

On the other hand, skilled writers usually write in styles that take longer to compose. Action and dialog take longer to write than narrative exposition, limited POV takes longer than omniscient, and a single paragraph of description can take hours to craft.

Furthermore, novices often skip planning and revision, while expert writers plan extensively and revise throughout the writing process.

Finally, writing researchers observe that higher quality writing takes longer to produce.[4]New writers tend to keep everything they write, while skilled writers often explore ideas they don't end up using, then cut some of their material.

[3] Anne Becker, "A Review of Writing Model Research based on Cognitive Processes" Ch. 3, pg. 48 (2006)
[4] K Anders Ericsson, "Toward a general theory of expertise", 1991

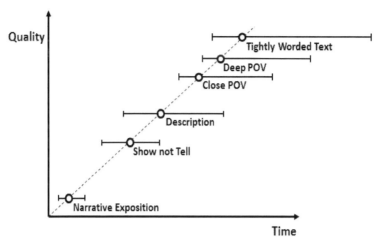

Skilled craftsmanship takes time

Some Genres Take Longer

The genre in which you write can also affect writing speed. Romance novels are said to be the faster to write in terms of words per day. Science Fiction and Fantasy both take longer, probably because they both require world building.

Action-Adventure and Mysteries are plot-based. They need extra time to plan events and timelines and for structural revision later.

Science Fiction and Fantasy both require world building, a planning activity that occurs either in the author's head or during free writing.

Historical fiction requires extra time for research, to recreate a historical time and place.

Romance and horror Deeply emotional genres, often require additional time for surface revision. Since the emotional content of a story lies in the wording, these genres often need extra time for crafting language at the surface level.

I'm a Fantasy writer, one of the slower genres, just one more thing that contributes to my slow writing speed.

2. Perception - Two Measures of Writing Speed

There's also a matter of perception. You may believe your writing is unbearably slow compared to other people, but it may be that you're comparing your overall or finished speed to their drafting speed. When calculating your own writing speed, it's important to understand the difference between drafting speed and finished speed, and to have a sense of what's normal for each.

Writers trying to increase their writing speed typically aim for numbers like 1,000-2,000 words a day. That's fast, but it's an attainable goal. It's said to be the speed professional writers working full time typically achieve. It's important to understand what the numbers mean.

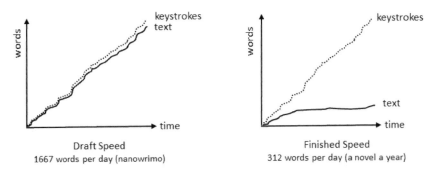

Draft Speed
1667 words per day (nanowrimo)

Finished Speed
312 words per day (a novel a year)

Writing speed – draft vs. overall[5]

Drafting speed

As a benchmark, consider NaNoWriMo, the National Novel Writing Month contest held in November, in which contestants try to write an entire novel in a single month. To complete NaNoWriMo, a contestant must produce 50,000 words in 30 days, or an average of 1667 words a day.
The rules allow participants to plan beforehand, and writers often revise their work after the contest closes. Presumably most of the text submitted for NaNoWriMo is draft.

---

[5] InputLog, copyright Marielle Leijten and Luuk Van Waes, University of Antwerp

Draft means putting words on paper as quickly as possible. When you're drafting, you're allowed to write badly. Narrative exposition is fine. Omniscient POV is fine. Info dumps, awkward sentence structure, and stilted dialog are all fine. Clichés are great because they convey a lot of information in just a few words. Things you aren't allowed to do in polished writing are welcome in draft, where your only mission is to get the story down as fast as you can.

Even when writing draft, 1667 words a day is a difficult goal. Not everyone can do it.

Finished Speed

What about the writing speed for finished work? A professional novelist can usually produce a novel in a year. A typical novel has 90,000 words. If the novelist worked six days a week for a year, that would be 287 days, or 312 words per day.

A novel a year

words	90,000
writing days	287
words a day	312

Words per day for finished work

Why so slow? Because drafting accounts for only around 18% of all the time spent writing. Finished writing consists of a number of phases, plan, draft, revise, and polish. For skilled writers, drafting takes up less than a fifth of overall writing time.

This profile is highly individual, and varies from one writer to another. It also varies for different types of writer. Planners spend more doing formal planning, while Pantsers spend more time in revision.

The profile of time spent in each phase of writing also varies for different genres.

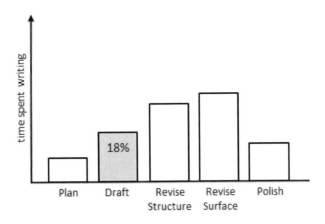

Time spent in each phase of writing

3. Inefficiency

Beginners use everything they write, but experienced writers generate about five times as much material as goes into the finished manuscript. That means that, for every page kept, four are thrown away. For some writers, or some passages, it could be as high as ten to one.

What inefficiency looks like

There are all sorts of reasons to delete text into which you've put considerable time and effort:

- o   You delete a scene.
- o   You have to change to beginning of the story to make it consistent with later developments.
- o   You move a scene, breaking the transitions.
- o   You remove a prologue, someone told you editors hate them.
- o   You remove a subplot.
- o   You remove an info-dump.
- o   You thin out some material to speed up the pacing.
- o   You merge characters or plot points.

For whatever reason, a passage just doesn't work and you're forced to "murder your darlings", a situation that comes up so often it was given a cool name. It can happen for a number of reasons: the passage was description-heavy and distracted from the action, it focused on something that wasn't important, or it created a logical inconsistency. In my own case, for "logical inconsistency" read "bone-headed error".

I once wrote a work of fan fiction that included a description of the view from the highest level of a tower guarding the road through a mountain pass. The passage captured the feel of the wind high up in the air, the hawks wheeling just overhead, and the sickening drop to the road below.

When it was finished, I leaned back and regarded my work with satisfaction. Then I realized that when the scene took place, the tower hadn't been built yet.[6] The first stone wouldn't be laid for another seven years, when the invaders returned home and raised it to block the exit behind them.

The timeline was canon, it couldn't be changed. Epic fail on my part. No matter how beautifully written the description was, the watchtower had to go. My POV character found himself standing on the road itself and camping beside it after the tower was deleted.

Cutting text for whatever reason is painful, but it's part of writing. Most writers would prefer a strategy that results in cutting less.

The limits of efficiency

There are two kinds of inefficiency in writing: ordinary inefficiency, and that which is necessary for the creative process.

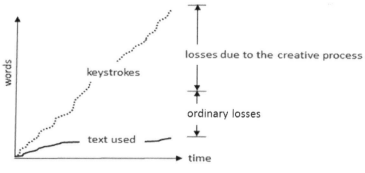

Efficiency in writing

---

[6] The tower was Cirith Ungol, and the story began on the first day of the War of the Last Alliance, in SA 3434. Cirith Ungol wouldn't be built until after the war ended in SA 3441, seven years later. Oops.

It's possible to write more efficiently, but only up to a point.[7] Writing is a creative activity, and inherently inefficient. When you write, you try out new things and explore ideas you may or may not use. Much of the material you type in won't make the final manuscript. It gets worse with time, the more experience you gain as a writer, the more material you'll cut.

Type 1 - Ordinary Losses

Ordinary losses are the result of work habits that result in wasted effort without adding quality to the finished product. Most of ordinary losses are due to one of two culprits:

o   Doing things in the wrong order
o   Perfectionism

To illustrate the danger of doing things in the wrong order, I offer the following cautionary tale.

Example - Tearing Up Fifth Avenue

I went to school in Pittsburgh, and I had to cross Fifth Avenue on my way to Physics classes or medieval reenactment events. The city is famous for potholes, some of which could swallow a Honda Civic whole.

Finally, the city repaired Fifth Avenue. It took a long time, but when they were done, the scarred roadbed lay beneath a new surface of asphalt, perfectly smooth and oiled a shiny black. A week later, they tore it up to install a new water main. Years later, I still remember how much I enjoyed mocking the city planners.

And then I realized this is my writing process. I fix typos and spelling errors when type the rough draft. I rearrange scenes and destroy carefully worked transitions. I spend hours crafting lyrical phrases in passages that are cut later. I change the structure, and have to do the word polishing and copy editing all over.

---

[7] I wrote what I thought was a terrific passage describing avoidable and unavoidable losses in terms of Carnot efficiency from the First Law of Thermodynamics, but my editor made me take it out. "Your target audience has a Liberal Arts education. Not only are they unfamiliar with the First Law of Thermodynamics, they probably paid good money to avoid it."

Have you ever spent a great deal of time crafting the dialog and action in a scene, writing vivid passages of description, then line editing the text? Then you changed the order of the obstacles and had to rewrite the transitions. Then during structural revision, you cut the whole scene. Painful and inefficient, and for many of us, the normal way to write.

Perfectionism may be the driver behind doing things out of order. In writing a rough draft, the impulse to correct spelling and grammar or to fix the wording can be overwhelming, even if you know you're investing time in something that isn't guaranteed to make the final cut. In my own surveys of writers, I found that every single person who identified themselves as a slow writer was also a perfectionist.

Type 2 – Losses Necessary for the Creative Process

In developing new material for your story, it's normal to come up with a variety of ideas, some good, some less good. You pick a few that serve your purpose, or that fit together well, or that you especially liked. The rest go unused, even ones that were pretty decent.

Writers are like artists. An artist might make a series of sketches, most of which end up crumpled and tossed in the corner. Perhaps a few turn out well, and one among them might become the basis of a finished work.

Were the sketches the artist threw away wasted? Technically yes, in that it took time to draw something that ultimately didn't get used. Could the artist have made the finished drawing without having made the sketches that got crumpled up and thrown out? Probably not. Very often the final, successful work is a product of the focused attention that went into the sketches preceding it. You have to try things out to see what works.

Consider what happens in a brainstorming session. Brainstorming is a technique in which a group of people come up with random ideas and bounce them off each other. It's uninhibited and silly, and a whole lot of fun. Usually, the session produces a whole lot of ideas that are pretty lame, but it also yields one or two that are really good.

Example – What to do with a captured vampire?

In my writing group recently, someone brought in a scene he'd been working on but hadn't finished because he didn't know how it should end.

The scene opened as follows:

> *A vampire hunter employed by the church had just captured a 500-year-old vampire, a particularly experienced and cunning example of its kind, and was preparing to turn it over to his employer, the Bishop.*
>
> *The Bishop wished to speak with the creature for what the hunter suspected were self-interested and sinister reasons.*
>
> *The hunter would have preferred to kill the thing outright. Even caged and chained, it was extremely dangerous. His loathing for them is personal, his own wife had been taken by vampires, and he himself had to stake her. It galled him to leave one alive.*

We wanted to know what happened next, but the author didn't know. We kicked around some ideas.

- Would the vampire lure the hunter too close to the cage, perhaps using its hypnotic powers?
- Why did the Bishop want to talk to the vampire? Did he seek vampire-like immortality, or was he planning to sic the vampire on someone else?
- If the hunter freed the vampire, would it foil the bishop's evil scheme? (whatever it was)
- Might the hunter starve the vampire, then trap the Bishop in the cage with it?
- When the vampire was set free, would it go after the hunter?

In a few minutes, we came up with at least half a dozen story ideas. Obviously they couldn't all be used. They differed in quality or verisimilitude, and they took the story in different directions.

Your first idea is almost never as good as your best among ten. Getting one really good idea may mean throwing out a lot of bad ones, but it's how you get that one really good idea.

How to Write Faster

You will write faster if you do the steps in the right order. You don't need to use outlines and beat sheets to write efficiently, you just have to exercise a little discipline.

If you write your first draft and spend a lot of time on action, dialog, and description, then kill that scene entirely because it was about something in the plot that ended up not happening, that's like doing a really good job paving the street before the trench for the water main was dug.

Every one of the examples of cut text fell under the heading of "Revise structure before surface". Unfortunately, PDR doesn't help 'bone-headed error' like getting the timeline wrong, but it's good for most of the others.

Plan, Draft, Revise

Plan, Draft, Revise (PDR) is a writing strategy can make you faster because it lets you be efficient. PDR constrains the order in which you do things: planning what to write, composing text, then revising its structure and wording.

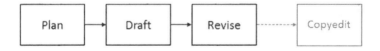

That's is an over-simplification, the process really looks more like this,

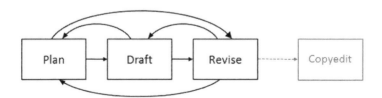

The message is the same, don't put a lot of work into something that might be cut later.

PDR is the strategy used by skilled writers to produce professional-quality text. It's also an efficient strategy the results in only your less-finished work being wasted.

How Does PDR Work?

Doing the stages in order is efficient. With PDR, you'll cut less of your polished writing, and you'll spend less time on repetitive tasks like copyediting and formatting.

PDR Reduces Waste

If you can minimize the amount of work that's cut, rewritten, or otherwise doesn't get used, you can produce a finished manuscript in less time. Less waste means faster writing. PDR limits the following practices, which are wasteful and guaranteed to slow you down. PDR limits practices that are wasteful and guaranteed to slow you down.

Editing while composing Don't try to draft and edit at the same time. It will slow you down more than any other bad habit available to you, and it's also the chief cause of writer's block.

Revising surface and structure at the same time Revising the structure and surface, meaning the organization of the text and the wording, at the same time is a bad idea for two reasons. It's very easy to get distracted from the turning points of a story when you're fixing a phrase. At the same time, the phrase you just perfected might get cut if the scene it's in gets cut.

Copy editing too early Don't polish the text, meaning don't copy edit it or work on the formatting, until the manuscript is done. This is a perfectionist habit that will slow you down terribly while offering nothing in return.

PDR can help you avoid these. You won't delete or rewrite as much of your text, so it will take fewer hours to produce finished work.

How to Do PDR

Work on the various stages of writing one at a time, and do them in the right order. Lather, rinse, repeat – it's a recursive process, something you repeat but on a smaller scale each iteration.

Plan what you're going to write By knowing more or less where you're going, you can avoid going into a blind alley or painting yourself into a corner, writing that you'll end up deleting in revision.

Don't edit and compose at the same time It's very likely that editing done early, particularly editing involving typos and spelling correction, will be overwritten in later revisions. Any copy editing you do while drafting is likely to be wasted effort.

Revise structure If you do your structural revisions on text that was written quickly, you can avoid cutting or breaking writing on which you spent a lot of time.

Polish Wording When you work on your text to get the wording just right, postpone copy editing until the document is finished. That way, the copy editing work won't be overwritten by a later revision.

Copyediting plus formatting, typos, and minor corrections must be done last, after everything else is finished. There's nothing more wasteful than spending time polishing something you later throw out.

PDR constrains the order you do things such that you don't waste any more finished work than necessary. The inefficiencies PDR helps you avoid are "Don't compose and edit at the same time" and "Don't do structural and surface revision at the same time". In both cases, separating those processes cuts waste significantly.

Copyediting and formatting are outside of the PDR process, and if you can stand it, should not be done until the manuscript is finished. Doing them while you're still writing results in a great deal of effort wasted.

What Will PDR Do For Me?

It's not just about getting things done faster. It's about not having to destroy the work of your own hands, which is always painful.

You'll Write Faster

PDR will let you write faster without interfering with the creating process.

You'll avoid the pain of throwing out finished work

Wasting work you spent a lot of time on costs you more than the hours you invested in it. It's painful to trash your own work. The less finished work you throw out, the less pain you suffer for the loss of it.

Time spent on each phase of writing

An estimate of time is spent in each phase of writing shows that revision takes up the greatest part.

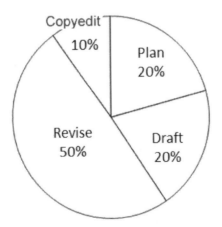

Time spent in each phase of writing

If structural and surface revision are broken out as two separate phases, each one by itself still takes more time than any of the others.

If you do the stages in order, you'll throw out less of your work, and more of your writing will make it into the finished manuscript.

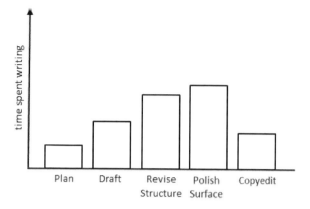

Time spent in each phase of writing

The allocation of time among the phases is highly individual, and varies a great deal from person to person.

It also varies from one genre to another. Romance novels are said to be the faster to write in terms of words per day. Science Fiction and Fantasy both take longer, probably because they both require world building.

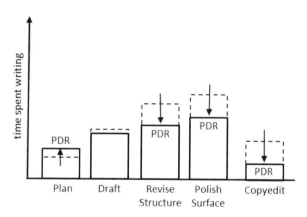

Time spent in each phase of writing using PDR

Example – Cutting Room Floor

Here's something I wrote that didn't make it into the finished manuscript.

> *"Why do you do this? Do you really need to buy baubles you can't afford on a kitchen maid's wages?" he asked the plain-featured barmaid as she led him up the stairs.*
>
> *"Six months ago, my dad was working on a boat when a surge in the harbor, the wake of a large ship, lifted the boat unexpectedly, and his leg was crushed between the deck and the underside of the pier.*
>
> *"He was brought home with his leg shattered, blood everywhere. We had little money, but without the doctor, he'd have died. So that evening, when I was supposed to be waiting tables, I went upstairs with a man I didn't know. In fifteen minutes, I'd earned enough to pay the doctor's fee. There were more doctors' visits the weeks that followed, and each one meant another trip upstairs. His leg mended eventually, but the accident left him crippled. He couldn't work, and we couldn't pay our rent. The landlord said he would throw us out in the street, so Mum was going to pull the little ones out of school. There's always work at the rug weaving shops, especially for young eyes and tiny fingers. But since I'm doing this, we still have our cottage, and the little ones are still in school."*

I was pleased with what I'd written. Then someone in my writing group pointed out, "You could just say her father was crippled in the accident and couldn't work anymore. It would completely explain why she's doing what she's doing."

They were right. As much as I'd enjoyed crafting the description, the passage neither advanced the plot, developed an important character, or imparted information the reader would need later.

I cut the passage and replaced it with a single sentence. If I'd left it in draft form rather than spend time revising and polishing it, I wouldn't have minded so much when I had to delete it.

Strategies for Planners

"Begin with the end in mind."

Stephen Covey

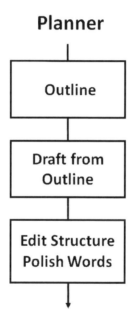

Planners like to outline. They get their best ideas before they start writing, and their stories are often plot-driven.

Planner Planning

*"The plan is not cast in stone. No plan
survives contact with the enemy."*

Field Marshal Helmuth von Moltke

Planning as Sketching

*"You should figure out (ideas) as you're writing them, just as painters
and architects do. We need (a medium) that lets us scribble and smudge
and smear."*[8]

Paul Graham, programmer and artist

Planning has two parts. First you identify a goal, and then you figure
out how to reach it.[9]

If the goal is to write a short story and publish it in a magazine, the
means to reach it might include selecting a sub-genre, reading stories
that have been well-received by the target audience, picking a length,
and identifying an interesting theme to write about.

Planning is done in a malleable media, while the activity being planned
is not. An architect designs a building using paper and drafting tools,
but the building itself will be built from brick and concrete. If you
want to move a wall, it's less expensive to do it early when the wall is a
line on a piece of paper, rather than waiting until after it's been built.

---

[8] Paul Graham, "Hackers and Painters" May 2003
[9] John R Hayes and Jane Gradwohl Nash, *"On the nature of planning in
writing"*, chapter 2, The Science of Writing, 1996

Also, things don't have to be planned in any particular order. You can plan a trip backwards, even though you can only take a trip forward.

Paul Graham, an artist as well as a programmer, describes sketching as a way to record and work through ideas.

The concept of sketching is used in a number of fields, drawing and painting of course, but also in architecture, musical composition, computer programming, and writing.

Before doing a painting on canvas, an artist typically makes a sketch to rough out the major features that will be in the painting. Sketches are used to explore ideas, and the artist often draws the same thing several different ways, one on top of the other.

The artist might make a number of different sketches, since paper is cheap compared to canvas and oil, and sketching is fast. The artist will create a lot of ideas that don't get used, but that's okay, it's the process. The important thing is to try things out and see how they work.

Story Goals

In planning your story, one of the first things to do is to establish who you're writing for, and why. Is your story supposed to inform, persuade, or entertain? Do you have additional goals? If you're like most people, your goals might include:

- To make money
- To get published
- To make people think you're smart
- To avoid offending someone
- To leave a message that will live longer than you will
- To prove someone else is wrong

At the same time, consider your audience. Is your story intended for young adults with a teenager's vocabulary and life experience? Or a specialized niche in science fiction, where your readers know every trope of the genre and have memorized the physics and worldbuilding. You don't have to provide as much backstory to these readers, but if you get it wrong, they will let you know.

What is your genre or master plot going to be? What tone will the document have, a self-help book that's chatty and conversational, or a novel told in deep POV without a narrator's voice? Goals aren't usually written down, probably because they're simple enough to remember. They may even be unconscious.

Be aware that goals, like text, may change during the writing process. In fact, because of the way one's ideas are shaped by the writing process itself, it would be surprising if they didn't.

Story Structure

"Learn the rules like a pro, so you can break them like an artist."

Pablo Picasso

Structure provides the bones of a story. It takes several forms, both the events of the plot and the turning points, how a character changes over the course of the story.

Structure occurs at all levels, the overarching shape of the whole story, the conflicts within a scene, and the MRUs (motivation-reaction units) within a paragraph or conversation.

The Three Act Play

The Three Act Play, a dramatic structure attributed to Aristotle, has become the basis of most stories and nearly every screenplay written.

I never look at my watch in the movies anymore because I've learned to keep time by the plot points. 'Clock running' means we're half-way through, just as 'whiff of death' comes at the three quarter point.

The structure consists of a series of plot points, spaced at exact intervals:

Incident > Stakes Raised > Crisis > Resolve > Climax

Readers seem to find the Three Act Play structure inherently satisfying, sort of like the golden ratio in architecture.

There was some discussion in my writing group about whether a preference for the golden ratio was hardwired into our brains or just something in our culture. Nobody knew, but either way, it doesn't matter. If an artist paints on a canvas that's 1.6 times as wide as it is tall, people will like his painting better. It's the same with the Three Act play. You don't have to use it, but if you do, it's what people are used to, and they'll like your story better.

This template gives form to a complete story with a beginning, middle, and end. The character is trying to do something, obstacles impede his path, and at one point he almost gives up, but decides to press on and fight to the end.

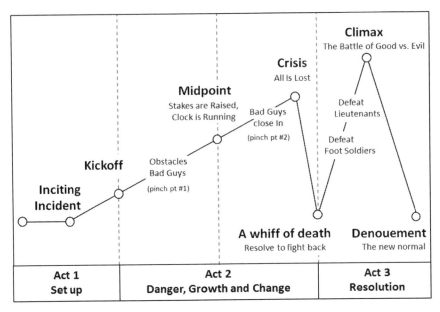

Plot Points of the Three Act Play

The major plot points of the Three Act Play are:

Inciting Incident The incident in the middle of the first act that first makes the character aware of the main story problem. He hesitates, sometimes he is scolded by a mentor.

Kickoff A second incident at the end of the first act that jolts the character out of his ordinary life.

Pinch Point 1 The appearance of adversarial forces in the form of obstacles and conflicts. Often the character is helped by friends.

Midpoint In the exact middle of the story, the stakes are raised and the clock starts ticking. This is the point at which the character fully commits to the story conflict, and begins to look forward rather than back.

Pinch Point 2 The return of adversarial forces, bigger and stronger than before, and with more knowledge about the character's defenses. Often the character is alone when they find him.

Beginning	Something jolts the character out of his ordinary life and motivates him to pursue a goal.
Middle	The story is more interesting if: - Obstacles block the character's path, either ordinary impediments or clashes with the enemy. - The stakes are raised. The rewards are greater, but the consequences for failure are worse. If the character wasn't so sure about this whole thing before, he's fully committed now. - Something happens to make him lose all hope. The obstacles are too big, the enemies too strong, or he's disillusioned, either with the goal or himself. - With nothing to lose, he digs deep and resolves to go on against impossible odds.
End	The character confronts the adversarial forces head-on, and everything is resolved, for good or ill.

Events in the Three Act Play

Crisis A false defeat late in the third quarter, and the belief that all hope is lost.

Whiff of Death A moment of despair at the end of the second act which fuels the resolve to confront the adversary and settle things once and for all.

Climax The final confrontation with the chief adversary in the middle of the third act. It follows a run-up through minions and lieutenants. Everything is resolved, and all loose ends are tied up.

Denouement Life returns to normal, or possible to the new normal. In a character-driven story, it's here that the character demonstrates that the changes he's made are permanent.

The Hero's Journey

Another story structure is the Hero's Journey, described by Joseph Campbell. Homer's 'The Odyssey' is a classic example of the hero's journey. The main difference from the Three Act Play is the emphasis is on the character, and the turning points that cause him to make hard decisions and to be changed by them.

When I surveyed writers, I'd expected the three act play to be the tool of the Planners and the Hero's Journey to belong to the Pantsers, but when the survey results came back, it appeared that both structures were used almost exclusively by Planners.

Tools for Planning Story Structure

There are a number of ways to plan the story structure. For Planners, that usually means beginning high level and abstract, then adding detail in successive iterations. The classic tools of Planners is the outline, but it's only one of many.

Storyline A one sentence summary, often called a log line. (Alien's log line was, "In space, no one can hear you scream.")

Synopsis A short summary of the story, no more than a paragraph or two long.

Outline An outline is a bulletized list. It's the most typical way to plan what one wants to say. Outlines don't require anything more than sentence fragments, so all your thought is freed up for organizing and evaluating ideas.

There's convincing evidence that writers working from outlines produce more successful text than writers who draft without planning.[10] More recent studies suggest that outlining works as well as advertised, but only for Planners who already like to outline.[11]

---

[10] Ron Kellogg (1988)
[11] David Galbraith (2006)

Concept Map A concept map, also called a Mind map, is a way to record your thoughts using circles and arrows. If the diagram takes the form of a tree structure, it can be written as an outline.

Here's an example for a concept map that explains the plan, draft, revise strategy for writing.

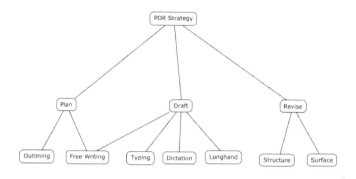

Concept Map as an alternative to outlining

Relationships among ideas are seldom linear, and tree structures are rare. It's far more common for ideas to be arranged in the form of a web, which explains why outlines can be so hard to write.

Treatment A short summary of major events of the story, sort of like a spoken version of an outline, sometimes with drawings and maps.

Beat Sheet A list of the beats in the story beyond the major turning points. A beat is any event that forces a decision or reveals character, there may be dozens of beats in a story.

Long synopsis A number of pages of narrative to flesh out the events in the outline.

Timeline A chart on which the major events of the story are arranged according to when they happened. It's used to present a character from having knowledge of or reacting to an event before the event has happened. Timelines help you develop plots that are more complicated than you could keep in your head easily.

Gantt Chart A timeline showing the start and end times of independent tasks.

Pert Chart A timeline with superpowers. The start or duration of an event may be computed from the start or end times of other events. Pert charts can help you to construct complex plots.

Scene List A list of each scene that will happen in the story. It's useful for making sure action scenes are followed by reaction scenes, and to note the placement of all the major plot points in the story.

Scene Checklist A list of everything normally included in a scene, the basic unit of storytelling. Scenes move the action forward and/or develop the character.

Butcher Paper Long rolls of paper on which to sketch the events of the story, usually arranged as a timeline. Events or observations may be written on sticky notes and moved around. Most people pin it to the wall or spread it out on the dining room table.

Index Cards A good way to jot down random thoughts and re-arrange them easily.

Pert Charts

I had just finished the most complicated plot I'd ever attempted and was complaining to my husband that my writing software didn't handle complex timelines. He arched an eyebrow and said, "Microsoft Project?" Dope slap. Microsoft Project is for Pert Charts, used to schedule complex projects.

Unlike Gantt charts, which show the schedule of different tasks with respect to each other, Pert charts compute the the start and end times of a task, or its duration, to the schedule of other tasks on the chart. Something changes on the timeline, other things change with it.

Pert charts aren't just for scheduling production in a factory, they're also excellent for plotting. For example, in choosing when a character will be rescued, it could be no earlier than the soonest his friends could reach him, and no later than the two days he could survive without water. Other time constraints might include how long it took to travel between two towns, how long high tide blocked a causeway, or how long it took for a drug to wear off.

Example – Romeo and Juliet, a plot with a complicated timeline

Shakespeare's "Romeo and Juliet" has the timeline:
- Romeo flees to Mantua.
- Juliet gets the sleeping potion.
- Friar John carries a message telling Romeo not to worry.
- Juliet takes the potion.
- Romeo's servant tells Romeo, "Juliet is dead".
- Romeo comes home and finds Juliet 'dead' in her tomb.
- Romeo kills self.
- Juliet wakes up, finds Romeo dead, and kills self.

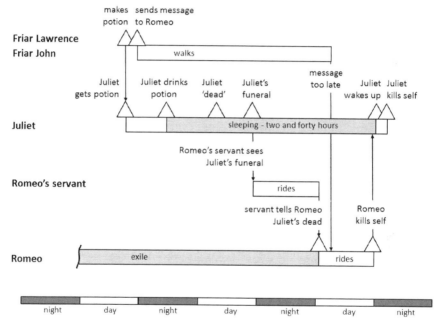

Pert chart of a complicated timeline

Note how the events are interconnected:
- Romeo must act on the message, "Juliet is dead" before receiving the message, "Don't worry".
- Juliet can't wake up before Romeo sees her in her tomb.
- Juliet can't wake up until Romeo is dead.

This plot is filled with events that depend on the end time of other events, or the duration of other events.

Anyone in the business world will immediately recognize Microsoft Project as the software application to create Pert charts. However, it's expensive, so I make the Pert charts in PowerPoint instead.

Fractal Decomposition for Plot Development

People who like to outline often begin their plots as a high level overview and from there, flesh out the details. Their planning process might look something like this:

Plan the story

- Write a one sentence storyline or short synopsis
- Write an outline
- Identify the plot points of the three act play
- Write a treatment or beat sheet
- Write a scene list

People who like to outline often build a plot on a single, high-level thought like, "Two cousins fall for the same girl" [12] to which they add a layer of detail, and another layer on top of that.

Until recently, I thought of fleshing out a plot as adding more levels of indentation to the outline. But then it occurred to me, plot development is like fractal decomposition. Fractals are common mathematical technique for generating patterns. To create texture, the main pattern is repeated, but on a smaller scale, in each successive iteration.

Stories are like fractals in that they have repeating patterns, too. A subplot can be a metaphor for the main plot, for example, a family quarrel that mirrors a civil war. A scene within a story might be a story that can stand alone by itself, because it has a beginning, middle, and end. Even a clip, a few paragraphs on the same subject, can be a story in miniature: a flashback, or someone telling a joke or relating a dream.

I felt so brilliant for thinking of it. Then I learned Randy Ingermanson invented fractal decomposition for stories ten years before I did, and furthermore, had done a better job of it than I had. So after traveling to

---

[12] *The Knight's Tale*, by Geoffrey Chaucer

Sweden to collect my Leibniz award for originality[13], I will refer you to Ingermanson's excellent blog[14] for the full description of the fractal decomposition method, and just touch on some of the highlights.

The principle is to start high-level and abstract, and to build onto the structure with each additional cycle. Start by telling your story in a single sentence, "It's about a sea captain obsessed with a giant fish."[15]

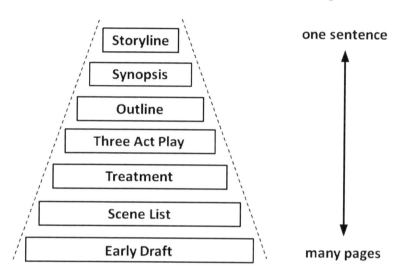

Fractal decomposition for plot development

These levels aren't necessarily arranged in order, for example, you might find an outline to be a larger document than a treatment. You might also want to do fractal decomposition using layers of your own choosing, like concept maps, beat sheets, timelines, and long synopses.

The point is to start with a high-level thought and expand it, one layer at a time, into the first draft of your story.

---

[13] Gottfried Leibniz (1646-1716) invented calculus, not knowing Isaac Newton had invented it ten years earlier.
[14] "The Snowflake Fractal Method" by Randy Ingermanson.)
[15] with apologies to Herman Melville

Scrivener for Planning

Scrivener is a software tool developed to take you from an outline to a first draft. Many authors compose their entire novel in Scrivener.

Begin by writing an outline. Let's say your major headers are chapters, and your sub-headers are scenes. Each header has a virtual index card, on which you can write your text. Unlike a real index card, there's no limit to how much you can write on it.

You can also write notes on the card, like the scene purpose, and whether it's an action or reaction scene. When you look at the cork board, you can tell at a glance what the texture of the story looks like, and if the turning points or beats are in the right order.

If you use memory prompts while drafting, you can use the split screen feature and keep the manuscript on one side, and use the other screen for memory prompts: a few bullets of outline, a scene plan, or photo. The reference material is stored in a folder separate from the manuscript, it won't be printed out with it by accident.

You can color code the headers to indicate degrees of completion: blank, a few bullets, notes to self, or narrative exposition finished draft. It's nice to be able to look at the outline and be able to see how close to done you are.

Scene Structure

*"Somebody gets in trouble, then gets out of it again.
People love that story. They never get tired of it."*

Kurt Vonnegut

The scene is the basic dramatic unit of a story. It can standalone as a story by itself, a one act play with a beginning, middle, and end.

A scene occurs in a single time and place, and is usually seen through the eyes of a single character, typically the one who has the most at stake in the scene.

Types of Scene

The scene must have a purpose. Either it advances the plot, or it develops the character, or conveys some important piece of information. In the first few lines, we must set the scene (show where we are in time and space) and establish who is the POV character.

There are two types of scene, action and reaction[16]. Actions scenes end in a disaster, reaction scenes show the character reacting to what happened and making a decision about what to do next. The two kinds of scenes are arranged back to back, with the action scene getting the reader spun up, and the reaction scene giving them a moment to recover before proceeding on to what's next, usually an even bigger disaster.

Scenes are containers for conflict. There should be as much confrontation or danger within a scene as possible, and the scene should end with a disaster.

---

[16] Action scene and reaction scene are also called scene and sequel

Scene Purpose

A scene must do something for the story, advance the plot, develop character, or convey information. If not, it shouldn't be in your story.

Elements of a scene include:

Scene Purpose To advance the plot, develop character, or convey information to the reader.

Set the Scene Establish where you are as soon as you enter the scene, also establish when.

Establish POV Normally the POV character is the one with the most at stake during the scene.

What's At Stake A scene is all about conflict, and there has to be a motive for facing the conflict and working through the obstacles.

Obstacles / Conflict A scene is all about conflict, and one way to add to the sense of conflict is to throw obstacles in the way between the hero and his goal. Obstacles can be physical, like flooded rivers, but they can also take the form information withheld or the hero's own lack of resolve.

Disaster at the End The scene must end with a hook, something that will keep the reader turning the page. In an action scene, it's a disaster bigger than any of the conflicts or obstacles in the scene so far.

It's best if your scenes contain all of these elements. If any are missing, your scene won't be as strong as it could be.

Action and Reaction Scenes

In a character-driven story, the reaction scene might be even longer and more exciting than the action scene that launched it. Consider the first act of Shakespeare's Macbeth. There was an event in the action scene, but the really memorable part was watching Macbeth waffle back and forth afterwards, agonizing over what to do, *"letting 'I dare not' wait upon 'I would'?"*

Action	King Duncan praised Macbeth but named his son Malcolm as his heir.
Reaction	Macbeth stabbed Duncan in his sleep.

Action and reaction scenes in Shakespeare's Macbeth

The decision came when Macbeth plunged a dagger into Duncan's heart. Reaction scenes end in a decision. They can contain much more than thought and contemplation.

Fractal Decomposition for Scene Development

Fractal decomposition works for scenes, as well. Plan the story structure, then plan the structure for a scene. Scenes may be developed from a few bullets, followed by synopsis, storyboard, and then may be drafted.

Plan a little, write a little

Another thing Randy Ingermanson advised was, "Plan a little, write a little". In my writing group, the novelists usually submit a chapter at a time for critique. The latter chapters might be sketched out, but they don't usually have the whole novel written or even outlined at the time they submit a finished chapter for review.

It's not necessary to plan the whole story, and then draft it from beginning to end. Most people know how the story starts and ends, and a few things that happen along the say. They'll sketch out the plot in an abstract way, and then flesh out one chapter or scene at a time. They might not even write the scenes in order.

However, I would urge you not to rework the wording of your text, and most certainly not copy edit it, until you've done the first structural edit and are certain the scene will remain in the story, and will remain in more or less its current form.

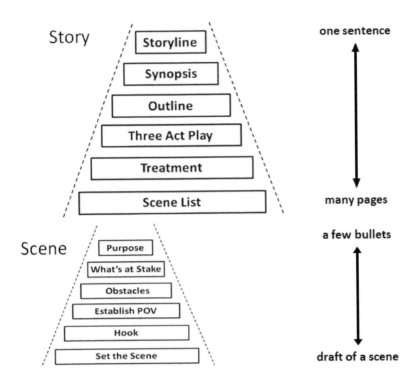

Fractal decomposition for scene development

At this stage, just focus on structure. Structural editing at the story level, and then at the scene level, should be complete before significant work is put into the wording.

Planner Drafting

"The first draft of anything is $#!"*

Ernest Hemingway

Clothe Your Structure in Words

If you're a Planner, the exciting part of writing comes before you ever set pen to paper. In the planning phase, ideas come quickly, the story takes form, and everything falls into place.

Once you finish the outline, it's time to flesh out the bones of your story and write the first draft. Planners sometimes find drafting a chore. They know how the story is going to turn out. They pretty much know what's going to happen along the way. The plot isn't going to change much between now and the final draft.

Translating visual images, sounds, and motion into words is one of the most difficult things we do on a regular basis. Furthermore, although we're hardwired to speak and to tell stories, we're not hardwired to write. Writing isn't instinctive and it's not natural, it has to be learned.

Drafting might be tedious, but it goes fast, and there's a certain satisfaction in that. If you know what you want to say, and you're writing narrative, the fastest of all writing styles, it's possible to hit 1000 words an hour. Even I've done 4500 words a day (once) when I was drafting narrative exposition, and I'm a snail.

You might also worry that the first draft seems like something based on a template, and isn't very original. That happens a lot, and it isn't something to worry about. There are only so many plots out there, it's the treatment that matters. Think of *"Romeo and Juliet"* and *"West Side Story"* Same plot, different treatments. In *"Book in a Month"*, Victoria Lynn Schmidt observed , *"A draft can be formalistic, but after revision, it is your own. "*

Drafting may be a chore, but you have to do it. As Nora Roberts said, *"You can't edit a blank page."*

Go in with a Plan

When you plan the overall story, you work with outlines and index cards, but when you start to write, you're usually drafting a scene. Start with the scene plan in hand, a short list of bullets, or a storyboard, and compose the text for a scene.

Before you write the scene, know what the scene is supposed to accomplish. Should it advance the plot, develop character, impart information? If you can't say what the scene purpose is, it may not have a purpose. That happens oftener than you may suppose. If you can't figure out the scene's purpose, you may have to cut the scene.

It's Just A Sketch

Generate text as fast as possible, always going forward. Don't go back to fix typos. Don't rework wording. If something about the story changes, go forward "as if" the change had already been made. Don't correct grammar or spelling. In fact, it's best to turn the spell-checker off.

Don't edit and compose at the same time, and never, ever copyedit the text of a first draft. You're also allowed to misspell words, use placeholders, skip things you don't feel like writing. In drafting, you have permission to write badly.

A first draft is not high quality, it's not supposed to be. It's a sketch, the first step in turning the outline into words. Don't worry about long, rambling sentences, the same word appearing twice in a paragraph, or failing to find just the right word. There will be plenty of time to fix it later.

Write in a Style That Goes Quickly

At this stage you have one objective, which is to get words on paper as quickly as possible.

Narrative Exposition

Narrative Exposition, or 'Tell', is the fastest of all writing styles and the one that most of us have been doing the longest. It lets you to get the story out quickly without having to craft dialog or description. You can change it to "Show" later, in revision.

Other techniques to speed up your writing include:

Omniscient POV It allows you to head-hop, provide information the characters wouldn't have had, and provide story information as needed. You can change it to limited or deep POV later.

Abstractions   Specific examples are more powerful, but they take longer.

Junk words If you find it natural to say "good" or "very", include them in your draft. The same with adverbs, go ahead and use them for now. You can substitute a stronger verb later.

Be verbose *"I didn't have time to write you a short letter, so I wrote you a long one."* It's easier to be wordy than is is to be terse. Feel free to ramble on without saying much, you can tighten it up later.

Passive voice Even though it contains more words per sentence, passive voice seems to go faster than active voice, probably because active voice requires more thought. Also, for some reason, present tense seems to go faster than past tense or past perfect.

Present tense For some reason, present tense seems to go faster than the past/past perfect I would normally use for narrative.

Clichés At this stage of writing, clichés are your friend. They contain a lot of information in just a few words, and you can be pretty sure that your readers will know what they mean. You can swap them out for more original expressions later.

Clunky wording Finally, don't worry about awkward sentences or clunky wording. There will be plenty of opportunity to work on them later. You can do this in draft, even though you wouldn't do it in the finished product.

Cut Corners Whenever Possible

In addition to writing in a style that goes quickly, learn to take shortcuts to avoid slowing down. Drafting is all about going forward without stopping.

Don't fix anything Whatever you do, don't compose and edit at the same time.

You can't be creative and view yourself with criticism at the same time. It causes writer's block, and it will do more to slow you down and almost any other bad habit of writing.

Don't fix your wording. Don't fix typos, grammar, spelling, or punctuation. Don't fix formatting. Don't fix anything, just go forward.

Put it off for later Sometimes you need to check a fact, or the spelling of a name, or you just don't feel like writing a passage just now. When you're drafting, it's all right to leave things unfinished. Highlight them so you can find them later, and keep moving forward.

Use placeholders If you need to write a scene that, for whatever reason you don't feel equipped to handle it at the moment, you can use a placeholder. For example, if you haven't given something a name but you think you will later, you can say [*name of boat*] or [*name of innkeeper*].

Similarly, if there's a scene you haven't researched yet or you just don't feel like writing at the moment, you can use a placeholder like:

[*insert battle scene here*]

Go back and work on it later, or brainstorm the storyline with others. Just remember to take it out before anyone else sees it, says one who routinely makes this error.

Free Up Short Term Memory

If you free up short term memory, you'll have more thought available for composing your story. Translating visual images, sounds, smells, and actions into words is one of the most difficult things we do.

Write in a Familiar Topic, Audience, and Genre

Freeing up short term memory means working with information you've known for a long time. If you're writing about a topic you know well, or you're writing in a familiar genre, then you have that much more thought available for composing the text.

Reduce Distractions , Clutter, and Interruptions

You may not think small distractions are eating into your short term memory, but they are. It's like having lots of apps open on the computer. Close them, and you have that much more processing power available, and you'll strengthen your ability to compose text.

Don't try to do two things at once   Don't try to multitask while you're drafting. Give your writing your undivided attention. Most people can't multitask, anyway.

Eliminate visual clutter   Keep an uncluttered work area. Some people do things with their screen to get rid of stuff on the margins. This doesn't work for everyone, but if it does work for you, it's good to be aware of it.

Don't live with other people   particularly ones too small to pour their own milk. Only kidding. However, getting up an hour before the rest of the household has many benefits.

Memory Prompts for Drafting

One way to free up short term memory is to jot down a few notes rather than try to keep it all in your head, or to have something in front of you instead of trying to remember what it looks like. Memory prompts could include:

A Few Bullets of Outline Jot down just enough to remind yourself of the major points you wanted to include. A few short sentences will do just as well.

Notes to Self A few bullets of outline or a few sentences to remind you of what you wanted to say make the task much easier.

A Diagram or Sketch Any kind of sketch, like a map, floor plan, diagram of a family tree, or a social network showing who knows whom, can contain a great deal of information. Anything on paper is that much less to keep in your head, which frees up that much more cognitive power for writing. [17]

A Calendar What date did something happen? How many days different from some other event? What day of the week was that? What phase of the moon? When was high tide that day? How long ago did it snow? Calendars can help you keep track of all that.

Drawings or Photos It takes thought and concentration to form a mental image of waves breaking over rocks, and even more effort to hang onto it long enough to write it down. Writing while looking at a photograph is much easier, and produces a more detailed and realistic description.

Words per Minute - Typing, Longhand, and Dictation

There are number of ways to record text when you're fast drafting. Type as if taking dictation, write in longhand, or dictate. The process of

---

[17] Short term memory and processing power are discussed in the 1980 Flower-Hayes model.

turning images and emotions into words is called translation, and it's one of the most cognitively difficult things we do.

Fast Typing It's possible to type very quickly if you don't stop to correct errors. To avoid the temptation to go back and correct spelling, you can turn the spell checker off. Some people even turn off the monitor while they're drafting.

Longhand One blogger particularly liked longhand for drafting because she was much less likely to stop to correct errors. Paper and pen don't have spell check.

Dictation Composing by speaking is faster than composing by either typing or longhand. While one would expect the speed of thought would be the limiting factor, and dictation would be the same 12.1 words per minute as typing and longhand, but it seems we compose faster when we're speaking than when we're writing.

I don't know why that would be, unless it's because we're hardwired for speaking, while writing must be learned.

Writing researcher Ron Kellogg measured the speed at which people could record word in each of three media, typing on the computer, longhand and dictation.[18]

Kellogg recorded speed for two different modes, reciting from memorized text, and composing new text of one's own. It was a clever experiment because it separated the rate at which one could think from the mechanical limits of how quickly one was able to communicate the words.

	Recite	Compose
Typing	40-90 wpm	12.1
Longhand	40 wpm	12.1
Dictation	200 wpm	29.3 wpm

Speed for Typing, Longhand, and Dictation

---

[18] Ronald Kellogg, "*A Model of Working Memory in Writing*" 1988

While typing is faster than writing in longhand, when you're creating new text, the rate for either longhand or typing is 12.1 words per minute. The average speed for composing new material while dictating is 29.3 words per minute, more than twice the rate for longhand or typing.

Dictation for Speed

I was reluctant to try dictation. I'd heard other people say they could compose more easily when they were speaking aloud, but I thought the whole thing would be awkward. I didn't want anyone to hear me stammering into the mike, or standing there with a deer-in-the-headlights expression when I got stuck.

Then I heard that dictated text came out more fluent and natural-sounding than typed text. I was struggling with wording at the time, so I was willing to give it a try.

Dictation feels different than composing with letters. We're hardwired to speak, we're not hardwired to write. When I spoke to compose, I felt like a barrier had been removed, and that I was closer to my story. I was composing better quality prose, and getting it right earlier.

After I got used to it, dictation became easier and more natural than typing or even longhand. My sentences became more natural-sounding, longer and more varied, and it's easier to find the right words. Typing seems slow and intrusive, like something is getting between me and the words.

Writing researcher Ron Kellogg (1988) found that, when composing new text, dictation can be done at more than twice the speed of longhand, or even typing.

Dictation is terrific for writing a first draft. I put on the wireless mic, then gather up some notes to remind myself what I want to say. They usually take the form of a scene plan, a few bullets of outline, a storyboard, or a few sentences of synopsis. I look at the screen while I'm speaking, to make sure the machine is turned on, and to deal with dictation errors as they come up. I don't necessarily correct them, I just say the sentence over.

Sometimes the words come more easily when I'm on my feet and moving around. If I set the screen display large, I can see it from across the room. It's not necessary to use the mouse, the dictation software lets you move the cursor by voice, so it's easy to replace or strike out whole lines.

Dictation is also terrific for transcribing notes. When the untidy heap of sticky notes, scraps of paper condom and random 'notes to self' on the backs of receipts grows unmanageably large, I can transcribe the irreplaceable collection of story ideas with uncommon speed by reading them aloud into the computer.

I often put story fragments into the rows of a table like a giant heap of factoids, and then sort them by scene or chapter. It works well and it doesn't take very long.

The Media Affects How You Write

The media you in which you write affects how you write. [19] When I sit down at the keyboard, I jot down badly-formed sentences and fragments of thought that can be reworked later. Word processing lets you do that.

On the other hand, when I have a tablet of paper in front of me, I chew on the end of the pen and think about what I want to say, and when I do start to write, the sentences are well-formed. And when I put on a wireless mic, at least after I've done it long enough to get over being self-conscious, I just talk. It feels like there's nothing between me and the story, and the words come out easily.

---

[19] Flower L. S., and J. R. Hayes, "*A Cognitive Process Theory of Writing*" College Composition and Communication, 32(4), 1981: 365-387.

Perfection Is Not Your Friend

"The story is always better than your ability to write it."
Robin McKinley

When I did the surveys to learn what fast writers did differently from slow ones, the single most important thing that emerged was that slow writers were perfectionists. Oddly, perfectionism didn't seem to improve the quality of the writing. It was the chief source of inefficiency, and appeared to add nothing.

Perfection has its place. It's a good thing to give your editor a manuscript free of typos and formatting errors, but you don't want to give that same level of polish to a rough draft or a block of text that will be reworked multiple times. Perfectionism has consequences, usually not good ones.

Example – Christmas Letter

A few years ago, I took the family Christmas letter to the office store to have it copied. When I got home, I noticed a small typo. The letter, which was color printed on both sides, would cost $100 to reprint. I couldn't stand it, I went back to the store and had it redone. I'd like to say this was an isolated incident, but it happened again the next year.

Here are some ways to beat perfectionism. As if I know how to give up being a perfectionist. I'm the poster child for what not to do.

Don't compose and edit at the same time   Whatever you do, you must not drafted and edit at the same time. Nothing will slow you down more. Nothing.

Turn off the spell checker   Whenever the spell checker flags a misspelling, I feel compelled to fix it right away. I get flagged by spell checker all the time, at least once or twice a sentence. It's not just that I'm terrible at spelling, which I am, but it's also that I write Fantasy and my character and place names make liberal use of diacritics, the little symbols above the letters.

Even when I knew I would probably rework or delete the text, I couldn't stop myself from fixing it.

It turns out that you can turn the spell checker off. I've heard that some people even turn the screen off. I personally don't do that, because of my habit of drifting one key over on the keyboard and not noticing right away, but if you can touch type easily, you might find that this works for you.

Oscillating This is normally referred to as happy to glad and back. I find myself deleting 'there', putting it back, and deleting it again. I also oscillate between 'then' and 'then'. In the draft stage, the exact wording just doesn't matter. I never really pin down my wording in till I read it aloud when it's close to finished.

Terrible First Draft Give yourself permission to write badly. One blogger suggested naming your file "Terrible First Draft" to manage expectations.

Murder Your Darlings Sometimes, when something won't jell, delete it. Cut it out of the draft and save it somewhere else.

When I'm working in Scrivener, I move the text I've killed to the notes section where I can still see it, and then I don't feel bad about having taken it out of the main document.

Have a deadline There's nothing like a deadline to forget being perfect and just get the thing out. The deadline doesn't even have to be real, meaning it doesn't have to be set by anyone other than yourself.

Flame Thrower Blogger Martha Beck urges that you think of perfectionism as something external to yourself, something dangerous. To that end, she envisions perfectionism as a socialite with an arrest warrant in one hand and a flamethrower in the other.

According to Beck, *"Long experience as a profoundly flawed person has taught me this unexpected truth: that welcoming imperfection is the way to accomplish what perfectionism promises but never delivers."* [20]

"My theory on housework is, if the item doesn't multiply, smell, catch fire, or block the refrigerator door, let it be. No one else cares. Why should you?"

Erma Bombeck

---

[20] Martha Beck, *"Reforming the Perfectionist in You"* in Oprah Magazine, July 2003

Planner Revision

"It can be fixed."
Noel Coward

Revision Overview - Structure to Surface

It takes at least three revision cycles to edit a story. On the first two, you'll revise the structure, and on the third, you'll edit the wording.

Revise the Structure

Whether you're a Planner or a Pantser, finalize the shape of your story before you polish the wording.

Example – Murder Mystery

Suppose you're watching a mystery program with a complicated plot with several red herrings, a large cast of characters, and a surprise ending. You have trouble keeping track of who the characters are, never mind how they're related to each other.

Then you watch it a second time. You know who done it, and why. You know who the victim is, and the murderer. You observe how they interact, and you notice the clues that foreshadow the big plot twist at the end.

Suppose, early in the story, you said someone was married to the barmaid. Later, you said he was single and spent most evenings in the tavern talking to her, but had eyes for a warrior princess who was passing through town, as well.

In the first read-through, you notice you've contradicted yourself. In your revision plan, you have to decide if he's a doting husband with a new baby or a young man with girlfriends all over town. Maybe you realize he's a middle-aged man with a teenage son, and it's his boy who's making sheep eyes at the warrior princess.

Pass 1 – Read through, form a general impression.

o   Who did you write your story for, and why?
o   How do you think your readers will perceive it?
o   The structure should be goal > obstacles > resolution. If not, it isn't a story.
o   Is the goal big enough for the effort required?
o   Is the resolution satisfying?
o   Does the character change?

List the problems, biggest first, with plans for how to fix them.

At this stage, we're looking for story level problems, where a story level problem is something that extends beyond the boundaries of a single scene or chapter.

A story level problem isn't necessarily a big problem. Chekov's gun, an object that was mentioned but never used, can be fixed by deleting the line in which it appeared. An internal inconsistency, like someone's black hair turned out to be brown, or their name was spelled several different ways, can be fixed by changing a single word.

With a revision plan in hand, you read through the manuscript a second time, specifically looking for evidence of the most serious problems. When you find them, mark the passages that need to change.

Pass 2 - Read through a second time. Mark what to move, add, clean up, or delete.

o   Are any major plot points missing?
o   Do events happen in the right order? If not, what should the order be?
o   If there are timeline collisions, what needs to move?

Make the structural edits starting with the largest, but don't fix the wording.

Don't just edit a single document, keep an archive of previous versions. You may cut something and want it back later, or change the wording and decide you liked the original better. While it's usually possible to reconstruct something that was lost, it's easier to find it in the archives.

Polish the Surface

One measure of skilled writing is that it sounds good when read aloud. When the text is spoken, you can hear any clumsiness in the wording that was invisible to your eye, and you think of phrasings that wouldn't have occurred to you at the keyboard.

Pass 3 – Replace draft text with well-crafted prose.

1. Replace Tell with Show to convey the emotions of the story. Convert omniscient voice into deep POV, passive voice to active, remove adverbs and clichés, and employ all the tricks of the writer's craft to manipulate the reader's emotions.

2. At the same time, replace narrative exposition with lyrical writing that's easy to read.

Polishing the wording takes longer than structural revision. If you're a typical writer, you'll have a Pass 4, Pass 5, … , Pass 12, etc.

It might be possible to revise a manuscript in just three cycles, but I have never done it. There are so many ways to keep on tweaking tweak the wording, and so many details that get added after the story was supposed to be finished. Online publishing, where you can make changes whenever you want. Gotta love it.

Avoid Waste

Revising from global level Structure to Surface is what experienced writers do, but the technique will also help you to write fast. A technique from theater costuming explains why it works.

Example – Muslin Mockup

I've been doing medieval reenactment for a long time, I first got involved in LARP, Live Action Role Playing, in third grade when I made Robin Hood costumes for the kids on the street and enlisted them as my merry men.

As a college student, I didn't have much money. My idea of a splurge was make generic macaroni with milk instead of water. Even so, I wanted to make a 12th century Norman cotehardie from German velvet, leather, and fur. Costuming materials were expensive, and I had to make them go as far as I could.

One day, I was sitting around with my reenactment friends knitting chain mail with pliers, when one of the theater majors held up a muslin mockup for the costume she was making. In theater, apparently it's standard practice to make a muslin before taking the scissors to expensive fabric.

Making a muslin is a form of sketching. You can rough out a sleeve, pin it in place, take a tuck here and there, and if it still doesn't work, throw it out and start over. You wouldn't do that with silk. Once the design is complete, the muslin is taken apart and used as the pattern. Armloads of muslin may get thrown out, but only a few scraps of expensive fabric end up in the trash.

Structure is the plot, Surface is the wording [21]

Writing is the same. The structure of the story is a muslin mockup, the finely crafted wording, which in writing is called Surface, is like embroidered silk.

---

[21] artwork by Rachel Fast

Surface is expensive because it took a lot of time to make. You don't want to waste any more of the silk than you have to, so you work in muslin as long as you're still exploring your story's shape.

Seven Levels of Editing

Edit is an overused word which means anything from correcting spelling to offering direction about the story's purpose. Most people first learn copyediting, superficial corrections to working like spelling and grammar.

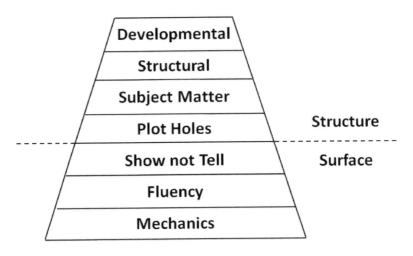

Levels of editing

With experience, they progress to editing for fluency (readability), internal consistency (logic), and finally the highest form of all, developmental editing (story structure, purpose and audience).

The process of revision is best done in the reverse order from which the processes were learned, from most sophisticated to least.

Developmental Editing is the highest form of revision. It deals with the story's purpose, also called rhetorical goals. These include: why the story was written, the needs and expectations of the readers, and what the story is trying to say. It also addresses things that should be taken out, or are missing. Look for what the story is trying to accomplish, and whether the material makes sense.

Structural Editing deals with the shape of the story at a high level, as determined by the events of the plot, turning points of the character arc, and pacing between events. Look for whether the story has the shape, "Goal > Obstacles > Resolution > Aftermath".

Subject Matter Editing / Fact Checking – For nonfiction, the subject matter of the document is reviewed for accuracy.

Even for a work of fiction, it's important to check facts. In historical fiction, dates should be verified and names should be spelled correctly. In science fiction, ordinary facts, like when you can use carbon dating, how long rigor mortis lasts, or whether gold tarnishes, should be used correctly. On the other hand, if you want to travel through time or bring someone back from the dead, you don't have to fact check.

Plot Holes, or Editing for Internal Consistency means making sure that events happen for a reason, and that what a character says or does should be consistent with his personality and what he's done in the past.

If you're writing science fiction or fantasy, you must follow the rules of your own worldbuilding. If someone who's undead makes horses and dogs uneasy, he can't ride horses or have a dog.

Editing Emotion Experience or "Show" refers to all the things that create the reader's emotional experience. When editing for emotion, look for blocks of narrative that could be turned into 'show', an omniscient point of view that could be given to an individual character, or for opportunities to add sounds and smells to a description.

Editing for Fluency means crafting fluent wording that's easy to read as well as lyrical-sounding. Look for awkward phrasing, repeated words, and ambiguous pronouns. Edit out junk words, and replace common ways to say things with original wording.

Mechanics which is also called line edition or copyediting, refers to grammar and spelling, punctuation, formatting, layout, minor tweaks to word usage, and writing style. Look for anything the spell-checker flags, proper use of past and past perfect tense, and proper use of commas inside lines of dialog. This is also the place to confirm homonyms were used correctly.

Delay Before Revising

It's a good idea to wait a little while between drafting and revisions. Most people allow at least a week, but a month is better.

Revisions done right away tend to be to the surface, revisions postponed tend to be global.[22] To revise efficiently, you must to do global (structural) revisions before surface. Therefore, you need to allow a cooling off period between the two.

Preparing to Proofread

When you revise structure, you skim large blocks of text for things like the order of events in the plot, a character's pattern of behavior, or whether the stakes are high enough to provide a motive. It's usually better to make notes on a pad of paper, chart, or beat sheet, because it focuses your efforts on a level above the wording.

When you revise surface, you're editing the wording itself. Since editing the wording involves striking out phrases, changing words, and reworking sentences, most people find it easiest to write on the manuscript itself.

Work In Hardcopy

If you're going to edit a hardcopy of the manuscript, leave yourself plenty of whitespace in which to write. Give the document wide margins, double space the lines, or allow extra space between paragraphs.

I recommend adding page numbers to the proof copy. That way, when you're taking notes about things to fix, you can write down the page number and find it later.

---

[22] Denis Alamargot & Lucile Chanquoy, *"Through the Models of Writing"*, 2001

Read Aloud

At a primal level, storytelling is meant to be spoken. Speech is instinctive, while reading and writing are not. There's something magical about reading aloud. You hear the overall rhythm of the sentences in a way you don't when you read silently, and catch things you wouldn't have caught otherwise: missing words, sentence fragments, and repeated words used too close together.

Have Someone Read To You (even a computer)

I find that reading only works if I read to other people. If I read aloud to myself, I get lazy, and before I finish the first page, I fall silent and start skimming, seeing what I want to see rather than what's on the page. That's not helpful.

Have the computer read aloud to you. It may have a robot voice, but you'll still get the benefit of hearing how your wording sounds.

Revise Story Structure

"I've found the best way to revise your own work is to pretend that somebody else wrote it and then to rip the living s%#! out of it."

Don Roff

One of the chief skills of an expert writer is the ability to diagnose and fix common problems. [23]

Pass 1 - Inspect the Story Structure

Start by reading the manuscript from beginning to end to form an overall impression. If you're visually oriented, you might want to keep a diagram of the Three Act Play nearby, and make a sketch of the timeline.

You can jot down notes, but don't write on the manuscript. If you do, you'll be tempted to edit the wording. That is not your task at the moment. Right now, you're observing the purpose, organization, and tone of your story.

What Is the Story's Purpose?

- o What are you trying to say, and to whom?
- o Is the writing style appropriate to audience?

Ask yourself if, based on content and organization, your audience will be able to understand what you're trying to say.

Is the Story Broken?

- o Is it a story? Does it have a beginning, middle, and end?
- o The main character doesn't change.
- o The main character isn't likable, or worse, isn't interesting.
- o The tone doesn't agree with the theme.
- o The story question isn't answered at the end.

---

[23] Linda Flower, John R. Hayes, L Carey, and Karen Schriver, *"Detection, diagnosis, and the strategies of revision"*, American Psychologist, 1986

These are devastating problems. If what you've written doesn't take the form goal > obstacles > conflict, it isn't a story. This is also true if the main character doesn't grow or change.

The story is also broken if the main story question is never answered.

Example - Fangirl

(Spoiler Alert) *One of my favorite books is "Fangirl" by Rainbow Rowel. It's about a fanfic author racing to finish her epic "This is how the series should have ended" before the final book in the canon series is published. She's already invested two years in the project, but has fallen behind, and the deadline falls during finals. In the last chapter, we see her celebrating an academic success, but we never learn whether she finished her epic in time to scoop the canon novel.*

The problem with *Fangirl* was that story question was never answered. It was as if the chapter containing the Climax was missing, and it made me nuts.

Another major problem occurs when the story premise isn't believable. This doesn't come up often, as readers will suspend disbelief for almost anything. As a reader, I'm fine with magic rings, coming back from the dead, faster-than-light spacecraft, vampire boyfriends, time travel, and shape-shifting, which is not only supernatural but also violates conservation of mass. In fact, there's very little I won't believe in a story, except maybe keeping the Merovingian Conspiracy secret for hundreds of years, or going on a second date with Christian Grey.

If there's a pattern, I think it's that one can play fast and loose with the laws of nature and readers will accept that, but they'll never believe in characters who act differently than real people would act.

Even in science fiction and fantasy, there are things the readers won't accept. There's a particularly bad science fiction movie from the 1950s in which an alien steps out of the ship and says, "*I am speaking to you as a form of photosynthesis.*" Noooo! The thought of it still makes me cringe.

Finally, a story is broken if the tone doesn't agree with the theme. A tone that's "off" is deeply disturbing and can make the reader stop reading.

Example - Out Of Africa

When the movie first came out, Saturday Night Live did a skit in which a movie critic gave a bad review to "Out of Africa". "You call that a comedy? Her coffee plantation burned and he was killed in a plane crash? Excuse me, but I didn't think it was funny."

That example was a parody, but it makes the point. The tone must match the theme or the reader will find it so disturbing they'll put the book down and walk away. Imagine a version of *"Pride and Prejudice"* by Stephen King or Erma Bombeck and the lighter side of Kafka's *"The Trial"*.

Checklist of Story Structure Problems

Broken Story
- o   Goal not big enough to justify effort required
- o   Story Premise isn't believable
- o   Story question not answered

Structure
- o   No beginning, middle, end (not a story)
- o   The story problem is not clearly stated
- o   Doesn't follow 3 Act Play (assuming you meant to)
  - - Plot points missing
  - - Plot points in the wrong order
  - - Plot points spaced too close or far apart
- o   Timeline flaws
- o   Do all the loose ends get tied up at the end?

Character Development
- o   Character doesn't change
- o   Two-dimensional hero or villain

Logic
- o   Events occur for no reason, or an event lacks verisimilitude
- o   Hero & villain have no reason to cross paths
- o   Villain doesn't have an understandable motive
- o   Rules of magic/local laws/customs aren't consistent
- o   Inconsistent names, dates, descriptions

Plot Holes – Inconsistencies in the plot

The Three Act Play

Identify problems in the story structure first. Hopefully your story has all its parts, but if not, during the first pass you'll see what's missing. If you're visually oriented, you might want to keep a copy of the three act play template nearby, and check off the major plot points as you come to them.

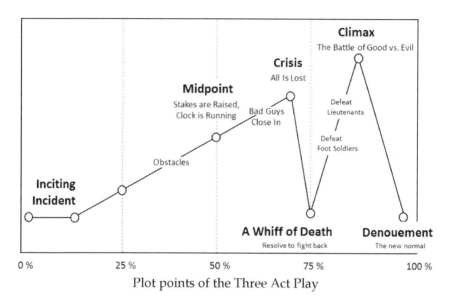

Plot points of the Three Act Play

Each of the plot points serves a purpose, and if it's misplaced or absent, it interrupts the dramatic structure that readers unconsciously expect. Here is why each of them is important.

Inciting Incident If the inciting incident happened before the story begins, it loses its power. Similarly, if the incident isn't important enough to propel the main character out of his ordinary routine, the story won't be believable.

Midpoint There's no point when the stakes are raised and the clock started ticking, such that the hero isn't forced to commit.

Crisis There's no point at which all hope is lost, often with imagery of death.

Climax There wasn't a climax, when the hero confronted the adversarial forces once and for all, or it happened offstage.

Dénouement The story ends abruptly at the climax. There's no denouement, the part of a plot-driven story where all the loose ends are tied up, or in a character driven story, the part where we learn whether the changes the character experienced are permanent.

Plot Holes

Next, look for minor problem like plot holes, logical inconsistencies in the plot. They don't always have to be fixed. Sometimes all you need to do to make the readers happy is "hang a lantern on it", or acknowledge you know it's a problem.

Internal Consistency The classic plot hole is that King Kong can't scale the walls of his enclosure on Scull Island in the 1933 film with Fay Wray, but he later climbs the Empire State Building with ease.

Timeline Errors Something that depends on the completion of something else happens before, information reaches someone too quickly, or someone travels from place to place too easily.

Options Not Considered In Lord of the Rings, no one thought to ask the Eagles to drop the Ring in the volcano.[24]

Character Inconsistent The character wouldn't have said or done that.

The Character Couldn't Know That An example of a timeline error. A character has knowledge they couldn't have had at that time.

Chekhov's Gun *"If you say in the first chapter that there is a rifle hanging on the wall, in the second or third chapter it absolutely must go off."*[25] Something is foreshadowed but doesn't happen.

Loose Ends Story threads are not tied up at the conclusion of the story.

---

[24] There was a scholarly debate on The Barrow Downs, an online forum, on this topic. They concluded, "If the eagles had dropped the Ring into the volcano, the book would have ended eighty chapters earlier."
[25] Anton Chekhov, Russian playwright

Deux Ex Machina In Ancient Greek theater, gods in chariots would be lowered to the stage with ropes and save the protagonist. The term refers to a situation in which the character is saved by an unlikely coincidence.

Make a Top-Down Revision Plan

At the end of the first pass, after you've read through and formed an overall impression, jot down the beginnings of a revision plan. Identify what the major problems are, and rank them from most serious to least. You'll deal with the most serious ones first, which you'll find be the most global in scope and will tend to require the greatest amount of cutting or rewriting.

Pass 2 – Mark What to Change

Mark up the hardcopy to show what needs to be moved, added to, cleaned up, or cut.

Please see "Pantser Revision" for an extensive discussion on using planning tools for revision, which covers tools for inspection as well as tools for structural editing.

See what you have:
- o A few bullets of outline
- o Synopsis
- o Three act play
- o Timelines
- o Beat sheet
- o Scene checklist

Move text around:
- o Index cards
- o Butcher paper and sticky notes
- o Scissors and tape
- o Scrivener

Fix the Story Stucture

Diagnosing and fixing common problems is one of the most important skills in writing. Experienced writers have a number of strategies for fixing problems.

In addition to deleting a flawed passage and rewriting it, expert writers might revise, note the problem and put it off for later, brainstorm it with someone else, or decide to live with it and do nothing.

Make the Goal Bigger

If the goal doesn't seem big enough to justify the effort put into attaining it, there are a couple of ways to make the goal bigger.

You could make the payoff bigger, but you could also increase the consequences for failure. For example, if it wasn't just the life of the hero at stake, but the lives of his friends.

You could also make the goal more personal. Suppose in *Diehard*, Bruce Willis had just been fighting terrorists. His goal, to defeat the terrorists, became bigger when he was fighting to save his family.

Follow the Three Act Play

Assuming you're structuring your story to the Three Act Play, and you identified the major plot point is missing, you'll probably have to write at least another chapter to fix it.

Answer the Story Question

A story is broken if the story question doesn't get answered at the end. The fix is to answer the story question. That might mean writing an extra chapter or two for the climax or dénouement.

Revise Scene Structure

"Failure is usually boring. It is the credible but unrealized threat of failure that is interesting."

Robyn D. Laws

Scenes are containers for conflict. Conflict reveals character. Without it, your main character is just someone minding his own business. In additions, scenes have certain conventions. In the first few lines, we must set the scene, which means to show where we are in time and space, and establish who is the POV character.

Pass 1 – Read through the scene to form a general impression, then jot down notes about major problems.

Scene Purpose The scene must have a purpose. Either it advances the plot, develops the character, or conveys some important piece of information.

Conflict Scenes are containers for conflict. There should be as much confrontation or danger as possible within a scene, and the scene should end with a disaster.

Common Problems with Scene Structure:

- The scene isn't set right away (time and place)
- POV is not established when the scene opens
- The scene purpose isn't clear. It doesn't advance the plot or develop character
- Tension doesn't increase during the scene
- The scene is narrative summary rather than action
- Unclear transitions between multiple POVs
- Not enough conflict
- Nothing (or not enough) is at stake
- The scene starts or ends in the wrong place
- An action scene fails to end with a crisis, or a reaction scene with a decision.

Draft a plan to revise the scene, beginning with the most serious problems. In general, the worst problem is not knowing the scene's purpose. Lesser problems include not having enough conflict, head-hopping, and misidentifying the most important character in the scene. Setting the scene and establishing POV are easy fixes.

Pass 2 – Mark up the hardcopy to show what needs to be moved, added to, cleaned up, or cut.

Fix the Scene Structure

Here are some common problems with the scene structure, and some suggestions for how to fix them.

The scene doesn't have a purpose

Delete it. If a scene doesn't advance the plot, develop character, or convey information, it doesn't belong in your story.

Actually, never delete anything you like. It may not work here, but you might be able to use it later. Cut it and put it somewhere safe where you can find it again.

Set the Scene

When the scene opens, say where the scene is set, and when.

Establish the POV Character

In the first few sentences of the scene, make it clear who has POV.

There isn't a POV character

The current fashion in writing is to stay in the head of a single POV character for the whole scene, ideally the character with the most at stake in the scene.

Writers sometimes switch POV characters within a scene, sometimes within a single paragraph. It's tempting to do head hopping in omniscient POV, where we can see everyone's thoughts at once. However, the reader forms a stronger emotional connection when there's just one POV character.

If you've made an artistic decision to do rapid-transition head-hopping, just be careful to make it clear whose head you're in at any given moment.

Add More Conflict

A scene is a container for conflict. If the scene isn't intense enough, there are a number of ways to increase the tension. You can tighten the pacing between conflicts, or you can make the conflicts themselves more intense.

Put the Character in Danger

Put the character in physical danger. Something heavy about to fall, a boat sinking, a dangerous person about to arrive.

You can also put the character in emotional danger. Put him in an argument, make him lose the respect of someone he looks up to, or have him be falsely accused. Have his girlfriend break up with him. You could also arrange for him to be blackmailed or emotionally abused, or locked in some kind of a power struggle.

You may not want to be mean to your characters, but remember: of text "unhappy characters, happy readers."

Withhold Something Important

Deprive the character of something he needs. His money could be stolen or his knife could slip from his fingers and clatter away, just out of reach.

Withhold information, like the location of a kidnap victim or a message that someone else is safe. ("Romeo, Juliet's not dead.") To create suspense, use Alfred Hitchcock's technique, let the audience knows something the character doesn't know, but should. ("Look behind you!")

You could withhold something emotionally important to the character, like love, respect, or approval.

Reveal Something Unexpected

Have the character learn something unpleasant. His fiancé is seeing someone else. His business partner has drained their bank account. He's adopted. Whatever it is may be old news ,but it's new to him and it changes everything.

Remove Options

With fewer options, the character is backed into a corner and his hand is forced.

Suppose your character is about to be tried for a serious crime. He's guilty, so he's not feeling good about the outcome. However, he has a passport and money, and he has an ex-girlfriend whose family owns a hunting cabin they never use. Then he realizes his passport expired last week, and the directions to the cabin are written on last year's calendar, which he didn't save. He now has two fewer options, and may have no choice but to stand trial.

Add a hook at the end

Give the reader's reason to keep turning pages. Scenes should end with a disaster or a decision. End the scene with a bigger hook than before. Confront your characters with some problem that seems insolvable, maybe not even survivable

Polish the Surface

"I make hammer marks you can't see, polish out scratches
you can't feel, and sell it for prices you can't believe."

A silversmith at Colonial Williamsburg

The surface of a story is made from carefully crafted wording. If structure is what the story is about, surface is how the story is told.

Structure is Muslin, Surface is Silk

As mentioned earlier, in theater costuming, when you make a muslin mockup, you're building a structure. With muslin, you can sketch. You loosen and tighten, move things around, change the shape. You can cut out a sleeve, and if it's too small, you throw it out and make another. You don't shed any tears over wasted material.

So before you take scissors to it, the shape of your story has to be worked out. You use the mockup to see how things fit together, rearrange the pieces, or cut them out entirely.

Surface is different. Surface is carefully crafted, it takes a long time to make. It's expensive, so you don't want to waste any of it. The bones of the story should be in place and not likely to change before you begin to clothe them in this expensive fabric.

Reader Emotional Experience
"Show not Tell"

"You don't write about the horrors of war. No, you write
about a kid's burnt sock lying in the road."
Richard Price

Readers usually read for an emotional experience, not an intellectual one. Surface has two parts, reader experience and fluency. Reader experience is everything that creates an emotional experience for the reader, like identification with the main character, or suspense engineered by drawing out events and shortening sentences as the tension builds. Creating the reader's emotional experience takes a high level of skill and represents the upper end of the writer's craft.

Show Not Tell Telling means saying that something happened, showing is describing it happening through action and dialog. It takes longer to describe something happening than to say that it happened.

Action A description of something physical that happens in the story, usually involving a conflict or a danger.

Dialog A conversation between characters. Ideally, each character will have his own distinct voice.

Description Description is an opportunity to bring the physical world into your story, and express images in lyrical wording. It allows you to place the character in a physical setting, which makes the action seem more immediate.

Foreshadowing Hints in the text that prepare the reader for events later in the story.

Grease the Skids Help the reader to believe something fantastical by mentioning it once or twice before it's vital to the plot. In the third

Harry Potter novel[26], Hermione Granger used a time turner to attend two classes at once (which developed character – it showed she liked to go to school). If the time turner had first appeared when Hermione needed to go back an hour to save the hippogriff, it wouldn't have been believable.

Abstract vs. Specific   Examples like "The forecast calls for two inches of snow by 10:00 pm" are more powerful than abstract ones like "They say it will snow tonight".

Action Tags   Replace traditional dialog tags ("Hands up!" John said) with action tags ("Hands up!" John released the safety on his Glock.) Action tags identify the speaker, but they also work another bit of action into the text.

Individual Character Voices   Give each of your characters an individual voice. A captain of the guard doesn't talk like a bureaucrat, and a peasant farmer don't talk like a scholar. Ideally, if you didn't use dialog tags at all, your readers should still be able to tell who was speaking.

Description Filled with Motion or Symbolism   Description is even more powerful when it contains motion. Consider a description of a dark, greenish cloud vs. the same cloud that's beginning to rotate. The storm clouds might also echo a character's mood or suggest that the character is dangerous.

Close / Limited POV   Close POV, also called Limited POV, is a technique which puts the reader inside the head of one character in a scene. It creates a more intense emotional experience than the reader would get from omniscient POV or from head-hopping.

Deep POV   Similar to Close POV, but deeper inside the character's head, and harder to write. In Deep POV, you can't name emotions ("He was in a towering rage"), you can only describe physical reactions to them. ("His heart hammered, and he clenched his fists.") Similarly, you can't describe a character because the character already knows what he look like.

---

[26] *"The Prisoner of Azkaban"* by J.K. Rowlings

Method Acting A technique used by actors to summon up the thoughts and feelings of their characters to create a more realistic performance. A method actor can cry real tears on demand, or make a vein throb with anger. Method acting is also used by writers to good effect, particularly those who write Deep POV. By experiencing the thoughts and feelings of their characters, they're more able to describe what their characters are going through.

Memory Prompts for Description

At the same time you're playing on the reader's emotions, you're also crafting beautifully worded text. The two are so dependent on well-crafted wording, they're best done together.

One of the major problems in writing is that short-term memory is that can be quickly overwhelmed, and if it is, it affects the writer's ability to compose new text.

Offload short-term memory whenever you can. It helps to write about a topic or in a genre you already know well. That way, you draw on long-term instead of short-term memory. Another technique is to make use of information stored in the form of notes, images, or diagrams, so you don't have to memorize it. This frees up processing power for the very difficult task of composing text.

Photos When writing descriptions, particularly those meant to pull the reader into the scene, it helps to write description while looking at photos.

I wish I'd known that when I was struggling to describe wildflowers growing in an old lava flow. Later, I went online and searched for an appropriate image and found someone's vacation photo of Craters of the Moon National Park. It was exactly what I needed, a snapshot of yellow flowers growing from cracks in the forbidding grey rock.

There are an amazing variety of images online of forests, clouds, waves breaking over rocks, ruined castles, in short, almost anything you might want to describe.

Drawings Other memory aides, like maps, floor plans, a calendar, or a storyboard can be very helpful. It's as though when you're not working so hard to remember something, you have more brain power left for the difficult task of composing text from images, sounds, smells, actions, and emotions.

Artifacts It's also helpful to have examples of physical objects I'm trying to describe, like a dagger with a bone handle, a dip pen and inkwell, or a leather bag full of coins.

Example – Riding Saddle

My characters often travel on horseback, so I keep a leather saddle in my study, the girth buckled around a sawhorse and the stirrup leathers shortened to the right length for riding. It helps me describe the creak of leather, the feel of the stirrup irons. As an added benefit, the children climb on it and talk to me while I'm trying to work.

Collecting artifacts is a useful practice for a writer. Whatever it is, you can probably find it online. Just learn to ignore the comments of other members of your household.

Example - Chains

I was writing a story in which my protagonist was taken prisoner and chained to a dungeon wall awaiting interrogation. I wanted to describe how the locking mechanism worked. Did the chains clink when he turned over in his sleep? Were the manacles still cold on his wrists after he'd been wearing them for a while?

I did some shopping online, and a few days later, a box arrived on the doorstep. I slit the packing tape and lifted out a pair of iron cuffs connected by a length of chain.

"Where did you get those?" my husband looked up from his newspaper, a line forming between his brows.

"They were on sale at Bondage Mart," I said primly.

He rolled his eyes and returned to his paper.

Blocking A technique from the stage, blocking means physically acting out a series of moves, usually for a fight scene or struggle, but it's also be used for love scenes. It's easier to do something and observe how it works than it is to try to imagine it if you haven't done it.

Writing Fluent Text

"Hard writing, easy reading,"

Nathaniel Hawthorne

One of the few measures of writing quality is fluency.[27] It's hard to say what fluency is, other than wording that's easy to read and pleasing to the ear.

Originally, all stories were told aloud. We seem to be hardwired to absorb them in spoken form. If your story sounds nice in spoken form, readers will like it better.

Fluent text reads as if it were dashed off effortlessly. You might have to rewrite a passage ten or twenty times to achieve it, unless you're Hemingway, who rewrote the last scene in *"Farewell to Arms"* forty times.

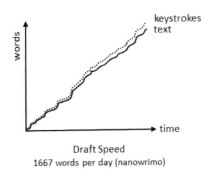

Draft Speed
1667 words per day (nanowrimo)

Finished Speed
312 words per day (a novel a year)

Lyrical Prose

Fluent text sounds good. There are certain mechanical things you can do to make your text lyrical like vary sentence length and pay attention

---

[27] The other metric of quality is length. Expert writers write longer pieces than beginners, even though their writing rate is slower. (conversation with John R. Hayes)

to the meter of sentences. Simple sentences usually sound better than complex ones, but crafting them is an art, and only your ear can tell you if it worked.

You'll need to have a store of material in your head, drawn from a lifetime of reading and listening to what goes on around you. Bad writers borrow, good writers steal. All writers pay attention to the work of other writers and are influenced by it.

Read Extensively

Writers are readers. One author advises that to be a good writer, you need to spend as much time reading as you do writing, both inside and outside of your genre. Another author says a writer needs to spend six hours a day doing some combination of writing and reading.

When you're well-read, you have a wealth of phrases, poetry, and passages of text in your head. They'll all contribute to the raw material from which you craft your own wording. *"Bad writers borrow, good writers steal."*[28]

Keep a Notebook of Lyrical Phrases

At Antietam Battlefield, there's a plaque with a passage from a diary kept by Cornelia McDonald, one of the nurses who tended the wounded there.

> *"All had the capes of their coats turned over to hide their still faces, but their poor hands, so pitiful they looked, and so helpless."*

Cornelia McDonald, nurse, 1st battle of Kernitch, 1862

I stared for a time, blinking hard. Then I wrote it down on the back of a gift shop receipt, and when I got home, copied it into a purple notebook from the children's school supplies. After that, whenever I read a phrase I wanted to remember, I added it to the notebook.

A few weeks later, when I was looking for something else on the Internet, I came across a frame from a Manga comic and was

---

[28] attributed to T.S. Eliot, but also to Oscar Wilde, and also to Mark Twain.

entranced by the artwork. The words with it were just as good. *"Now I shall see an end of him."* I caught myself thinking, *Wow, I didn't know the writing in Manga was so good!*

Copyright SelfMadeHero and Chie Kutsuwada
used with permission of the artist

The phrase joined the others in my notebook.

"Now I shall see an end of him, for my soul, I know not why, hates nothing more than he."
            William Shakespeare, "As You Like It"

"The debris cooled and went dark."
            Lou Lamoureaux, "Recalled to Duty"

" cut into rocks, the bones of the earth."
            Josip Novakovich, "Rust"

"His hair was moving gently, like weeds in water."
            Lorrie Moore, "Community Life"

> *"I am as practical as salt."*
>
> Stephen Schwartz, "Pippin"
>
> *" a breakfast of stale bread and green fruit."*
>
> Beth Sadler, "Taryn's Tear"
>
> *"What you know about women, I could juggle."*
>
> Jim Butcher, "The Dresden Files"
>
> *"I laughed so hard, tears ran down my leg."*
>
> Reader's Digest

If you want to write fluent prose, keep a notebook of phrases that strike you as particularly lyrical. Don't trust that you'll remember what you read. When you find something really good, write it down.

I find I remember the phrases wrong, for example, I recall the Cornelia McDonald quote as *"their still hands"* rather than *"their still faces"*. It seems right, their coats over their faces, their still hands resting on their chest, one ached with pity for them. If I were to use it in a story, that's how it would be. If "bad writers borrow, good writers steal", then 'steal' means to lift it and make it your own.

Take a Poetry Class

Some writers take a poetry class to learn how to craft their wording.

> *One of the guys in my writing group, a fireman and paramedic, took a poetry class to strengthen his already luminous prose. I asked him, "So, did the boys at the firehouse know about this?" "No, they do not," he answered primly.*

However, in spite of how useful they are, not everyone likes to be seen as the sort of person who would take a poetry class.

Rewrite a Passage Repeatedly

Good photographers take a great many pictures and throw out most of them. For many of us, the way to write fluent text is to rewrite it over and over. It's the process. The only writers who don't experience this are novices who neither plan nor revise. After putting that much effort into something, it ought to be for a passage you're going to keep.

There are a number of techniques for writing fluent text. When the wording won't jell, I find myself rewriting the passage over and over. Usually it gets better with repetition, but there's a point of diminishing returns.

> *It was the best and worst of times.*
>
> *It was the best of times, it was worst of times.* [29]
>
> *Times were good, or else they were bad.*
>
> *Times were both good and bad.*
>
> *Times were bad. Really, really bad. You just won't believe how vastly, hugely, mind bogglingly bad there were.* [30]

Rewrite a passage multiple times to make it more fluent

At first it would seem that writing something over and over violates the goal of being efficient, of not leaving anything on the cutting room floor. But reworking a passage to make it sound better can't be avoided. It's the process.

Write Text That's Easy to Read

> *"I didn't have time to write a short letter,*
> *so I wrote a long one instead."*
>
> Mark Twain

As a new writer, you might produce text with a 12th grade level of readability, but later, with time and experience, it might drop to the 7th grade level. [31] This is good. The more skilled you are, the lower the grade level your writing will be assessed.

---

[29] With apologizes to Charles Dickens, spinning in his grave at 300 Hz.
[30] With apologies to Douglas Adams, *"Hitchhiker's Guide to the Galaxy"*.
[31] The Flesch-Kincaid readability test outputs a number representing a U.S. school grade level. Microsoft Word comes with a utility to compute it.

Vary the length of the sentences. Don't place words that sound alike too close together, unless you want to do so for effect. Simple wording is easier to read, as is text free of junk words, adverbs, and clichés.

Simple Words   It's easier to write for graduate students than for eighth graders. However, if you simplify your text, you'll have as more readers and your wording will sound nicer. If your text is easily understood by fifteen year olds, as opposed to university graduates and above[32], your work will be easier to read and your readers will like it better.

Tightly Worded Text   Text is easier to read when it says what it has to say in the fewest words possible. Unfortunately, it takes longer to write seven words than to write thirteen that say the same thing.

Active Voice   refers to sentences that use strong verbs and avoid the passive verbs *is* and *has*. Readers like active voice better. An added benefit, active sentences tend to be short. There will be occasions when you'll choose passive voice, for example, when you want to distance yourself from blame. "Mistakes were made, butt was kicked."

Adverbs   In general, use strong verbs instead of adverbs. The exception is if the adverb contradicts the verb, for example, "She laughed bitterly."

The same applies to adjectives. They're most powerful when they contradict the noun, "an unpleasant reward" or "a scary baby".

Junk Words   Don't use words that take up space but carry little meaning. The classic junk word is 'very', but words like good, just, little, really, actually, extremely, or any of a host of similar words.

It's almost impossible to avoid junk words when you're drafting, but only use them in your finished work if you have a compelling reason, like you're writing dialog and that's what the character would have said.

Ambiguous Sentences   like *"Cheerleaders appeal to Principal"* or *"Kids make nutritious snacks"*. Don't make the reader stop reading to figure it out.

---

[32] As measured by the Flesch-Kincaid readability test, a function of syllables per word length and words per sentence.

Ambiguous Objects Structure your sentences so it's obvious which object is being modified. *"In Jurassic Park, a lawyer was killed by a dinosaur on the toilet."* Not likely. Dinosaurs are heavy, the porcelain would crush under its weight.

Clichés Clichés are useful in drafting because they capture a concept of just a few words, but in finished text, they have to be replaced with something original. It's hard to think up an original substitution, which is why we use clichés in speech more than writing.

Individual Character Voices Give each of your characters an individual voice. A captain of the guard doesn't talk like a bureaucrat, and a peasant farmer doesn't talk like a scholar. Ideally, if you didn't use dialog tags at all, your readers should still be able to tell who was speaking.

Choose One Item from a List Suppose we have a list of items supporting an argument we're trying to make. For some reason, readers seem to average the items rather than sum them, so the strongest item gets diluted by the lesser ones.

You can make a more convincing case by picking the best item and using it by itself, just as one excuse is more convincing than two. "I didn't realize today was the first of the month, and besides, I ran out of checks."

Wordiness Remove unnecessary words until the sentence no longer retains its meaning.

Choppy sentences Reduce run-on sentences, prepositional phrases strung together, and conjunctions. Read the sentence aloud to hear how it sounds.

Imprecise language Replace vague, abstract, or overly general words with more specific ones. Horse becomes mustang, foreign country becomes France, a man becomes George. Specific works better.

Stilted language Write like you talk. Everyday speech sounds better than stiff, affected, or overly formal language.

Express Complex Thoughts in Simple Words

It's harder to say something in a few words than in many, just as it's harder to say something in active voice than it is in passive. When I draft, I allow myself to use technical language because it comes easily, then I have to work to simplify it and make it fluent.

Why do people use complex prose? It's easier to write.

A passage from a technical paper,

> *"Expanding linguistic resources enables writers to become more fluent, since their selection of lexical and syntactical structures becomes more automatic."* [33]

may be written,

> *"The better your vocabulary and grammar, the better you'll write."*

Dictation for Fluency

This doesn't work for everyone, but many people can dictate more natural-sounding prose they can type or write in longhand. Speaking is an instinct, while writing has to be learned.

There's something magical about dictation. The only thing I can liken it to is if you've been typing or playing piano with heavy gloves on, and you take them off. All of a sudden, there's nothing in the way of the work you're trying to do. It cuts out the middleman. When I type, I work fairly hard to produce somewhat stilted prose. Spoken words are easier and more natural-sounding.

Whenever I get really stuck on a passage, I put on the wireless headset and say, "What I really mean to say is…" and somewhere among the "umm"s and awkward pauses, I get a passage that sounds just right, and nothing like the clunky stuff I'd been struggling to type.

---

[33] Denis Alamargot & Lucile Chanquoy, *"Through the Models of Writing"*

Anthony Tovatt[34] conducted an experiment in which he expected to see the dictation increased not only the speed, but the quality of the writing. The results were inconclusive, but even so, he believed it did, and I'm inclined to agree with him. My own experience with dictation has been that the text I've dictated is more fluent and more natural sounding.

Burst Pause Most people dictate in a series of burst-pause, burst-pauses, speaking an average of seven words before stopping to compose the next phrase. Expert writers compose longer passages, averaging twelve words at a time.[35] I personally can manage about three words, which says I'm bad at it, but even so, I've found dictation to be the easiest and most successful way to compose new text.

Speech Recognition Software Dragon Naturally Speaking is a popular speech recognition application for dictation. It lets you draft in a hurry, but it's also a powerful tool to use later on, when you want to craft fluent wording.

Speech Recognition Errors Keep an eye on the screen when you dictate. Speech recognition software is notorious for recording almost what you said, but not quite.

Speech recognition software errors

Dictation errors are different from other typos. The software returns real words, so no matter how wrong they are, the spell checker won't flag them. And if you do happen to find the error yourself, it's unlikely you'll be able to reconstruct what you originally meant to say.

---

[34] Anthony Tovatt and Elbert L Miller, *"The sound of writing"*, 1967
[35] John R. Hayes and Ann Chenoweth, *"Working Memory in an Editing Task"*, Journal of Written Communication, 2006

Spoken	Written
affixed to	a thick stew
you're in	urine
write and deliver	right in the liver
Tatooine	tatooing
sheer luck	Sherlock
written	Britain
intense	in tents
circumcised	circus sized
Lugbúrz [36]	love birds

Speech recognition errors

Dragon might transcribe *incident management teams* as *indecent management teams* or *he didn't like to show his emotions* as *he didn't like to show he's a Martian.*

Example - Painted Crab

Always, always proofread the text you dictate. There will be dictation errors, and the spell checker will not catch them.

I submitted a story to my critique group in which my character had a treasured memento from his childhood, a stone painted to look like a crab. Dragon heard 'crab' as 'cr@p'. I didn't proofread, so I didn't catch it.

The group must have wondered why my character made a prized possession of something most people would choose to flush. It wasn't until the hysterical laughter died down and they were wiping tears from their eyes that I was able to say, "No, a crustacean, a sea creature!"

On the plus side, it turns out that in moments like these, the earth does not actually open up and swallow you whole, however much you might wish it.

---

[36] Lugbúrz or "tower dark" is Black Speech for Barad-dûr.

I'm a big fan of Dragon and I use it all the time. Unfortunately, I'm a terrible proof reader. I once saw a title to a magazine article titled,

If yuo can read this, you mihgt be dyslxeic

Yes, I know I read things wrong, but for the life of me, I couldn't figure out what was the matter with that sentence. [37] Did I mention that I'm bad at proofreading?

If you're not much of a proofreader either, be aware of the hazards of using speech recognition software for dictation, unless you're not afraid to be a source of unintentional humor.

Example - Stinkbug

Another type of dictation error involves forgetting to turn off the microphone when someone comes into the room. Whatever you say to them will end up in your document. I caught this minutes before I uploaded it for publication.

The wind caught him full in the face, whipping his hair into his eyes, flapping his clothing like sailcloth. A sheer face of granite rose hundreds of feet above the road on one side, that's a stink bug, sweetie. It won't hurt you, DON'T SQUISH IT, just put it outside, that's right, a sheer cliff rose above the road on one side, a vertical drop fell away on the other.

Speech recognition software is subject to other technical difficulties as well, like microphones that won't turn on or jumping cursor, the tendency to insert new text in a spot other than where the cursor is placed.

Yet in spite of the glitches, I still think doing dictation with speech recognition software is worth the trouble. When I'm really struggling to say something and everything I type is awkward, I put on the headset and the words just come.

---

[37] Although when I drive with my sister, ("Turn left. No, no, other left!") it tends to cancel out.

Critique Groups

"If you show someone something you've written, you give them a sharpened stake, lie down in your coffin, and say, "When you're ready."

David Mitchell

I've mentioned critique groups before, and I consider them a crucial step in revision. After you've skimmed the manuscript and make notes about what didn't work, laid the pages out on a table and attacked them with scissors and tape, and filled all the margins with scribbled corrections, you still only know how you feel about your story.

You don't know how readers are going to feel about it until you let someone else see it. There's nothing like bringing it to a critique group to get a sense of how it will be received by readers.

The story doesn't make sense, they'll tell you. If the main character isn't likable, they'll tell you. If the story question isn't obvious, they'll tell you. If they don't remember a crucial piece of information you gave earlier in the story, do something to remind the reader of the important fact.

When you receive feedback, the only proper response is, "Thank you". Don't do what I do, which is to explain to them why they're wrong, even if they are. These people are your friends. It's so much better if they catch things than if an editor does, or worse, your readers. Those people may not even convey the information to you, and you won't have the opportunity to fix things.

Revision Summary

"Edit your manuscript until your fingers bleed and you have memorized every last word. Then, when you are certain you are on the verge of insanity...edit one more time!"

C.K. Webb

Things that take the reader out of the story

One of your goals in revision is to find and remove anything that might take readers out of the story.

Jefferson Smith, who blogs about writing, did a study of things that break reader immersion in self-published works. Every day, he began a new book, which he stopped reading the third time something took him out of the story. He then recorded what the three flaws were, and how many minutes he'd been reading when he put the book down.

While the typos and spelling errors common to self-published works were the most noticeable flaws, he was surprised to find that problems with story structure and storytelling were the main reasons he stopped reading.

He published a list of the most common things that break reader immersion, as well as an indication of how common each problem is. [38] For a new writer, it's an excellent tutorial on "identify common problems".

---

[38] Jefferson Smith, *"The 5 Most Common Writing Mistakes That Break Reader Immersion"*, August 26, 2014 from his blog, Creativity Hacker.

What breaks reader immersion:

Story structure: (plot)
o Implausible world building (physics, economy)
o Too little information to follow the story
o Characters floating through space without a setting
o Time flow – too fast, too slow, or without variation
o Deux ex machina an overly convenient coincidence

Story telling: (wording/fluency)
o Echoing – repeated phrase or sentence structure
o Poor use of language
o Dialog – unrealistic accent or historical word usage
o Using a word wrong
o Made up names for things

Poor mechanics: (copyediting)
o Grammar, spelling, typos, format
o Ambiguous pronouns
o Incorrect use of tense, particularly past perfect

from Jefferson Smith, "Immerse or Die"

The Process

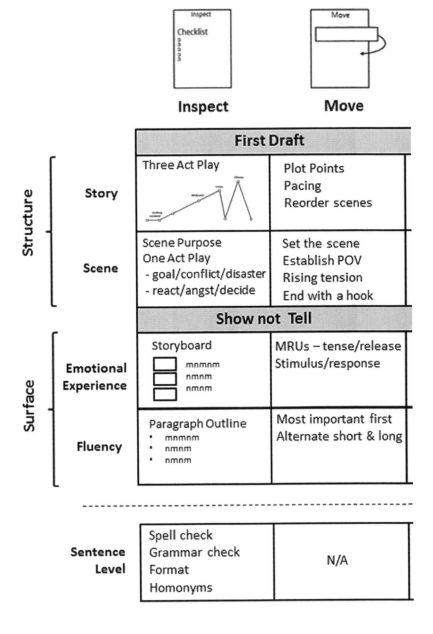

		First Draft	
Structure	**Story**	Three Act Play	Plot Points Pacing Reorder scenes
	Scene	Scene Purpose One Act Play - goal/conflict/disaster - react/angst/decide	Set the scene Establish POV Rising tension End with a hook
		Show not Tell	
Surface	**Emotional Experience**	Storyboard mnmnm nmnm nmnm	MRUs – tense/release Stimulus/response
	Fluency	Paragraph Outline • mnmnm • nmnm • nmnm	Most important first Alternate short & long

- -

Sentence Level	Spell check Grammar check Format Homonyms	N/A

# of Revision

Add   **Clean Up / Cut**

"What You Say"	
Obstacles Backstory Subplots	Motivation Internal consistency Events for no reason Plot Holes
More conflict - Internal - Psychological Foreshadowing	Unclear POV What's at stake? Too many characters
"How You Say It"	
Action / Description Deep POV Concrete examples Physical reactions	Info dumps Omniscient POV Head Hopping Passive voice
Simple language Use metaphors Replace clichés	Tighten sentences Adverbs, slang, jargon Junk words Repeated phrases

Revision Cycles

Rev 1

Rev 2

Rev 3

Revision

- -

Copyediting

N/A	Grammar, Spelling Punctuation Typos Format

Copyediting

"I edit my own stories to death. They eventually
run and hide from me."

Jeanne Voelker

Wait until everything else is complete

Nothing in this section will help you write fast. Everything here is
labor intensive and will slow you down tremendously. Yet you can't
skip this step, because polishing makes your manuscript ready for
publication.

Grammar and Spelling

The trick is to copyedit only once, and only after the manuscript is
completely finished.

Copy editing is also called line editing. That means fixing spelling,
grammar, punctuation, and typos. It also means making small tweaks
to wording, like "it's" for "its".

Spelling   Best corrected by eye, or by using the spell checker.

Grammar   In fiction, it's conventional to use past for present tense
and past perfect for past tense.

Typos   They're usually easy to spot when they're spelling errors.
However, if you use dictation software, the speech recognition
software only writes downwards it finds in the dictionary, so the
spell checker won't flag them.

Homonyms   Words that sound like other words, like there, their,
and they're. Sometimes these will trip the grammar checker, but it's
better if you can recognize them easily without thinking about it.

Copy editing can be done by someone else, and to some extent, by machine. The spell check and grammar check functions in MS Word perform a simple version of copy editing.

Usage and Style

Copyediting can also include checking to ensure that the text adheres to a specified set of style guidelines.

Four copy editors were killed amid escalating violence as rival gangs, followers of the AP and Chicago Manuals of Style, fought for control of the rules governing grammar and usage for American English. Near the scene, graffiti containing the word "anti-social" had been changed to "antisocial".

paraphrased from The Onion, a satirical newspaper [39]

It may be just grammar and usage, but there are people who take this stuff very seriously.

Format

Formatting includes the selection of font and font size, the use of bold and italic, as well as headers, footnotes, page numbers, indenting at the beginning of a paragraph, spacing between lines, and margin width. Text color is also a form of formatting.

Formatting also includes tables, embedded images, and Initialen caps, the large decorative letters at the beginning of a chapter. If the document is a large one, formatting may also include section breaks, table of contents, and an index.

---

[39] *"4 Copy Editors Killed In Ongoing AP Style, Chicago Manual Gang Violence"*, www.theonion.com, Jan 7, 2013

Layout

Your readers will like your story better if it looks nice and is easy to read. [40] If the details of font and formatting are under your control, it's best to format your work so it's easy to read.

Fonts For the body of the text, serif fonts, those that have an ornamental line at the top of the stems, are the easiest to read. Times New Roman and Book Antiqua are good choices. 10 to 12 point font is a good size for most people.

For headers, the cleaner-looking san serif fonts are a good choice. Ariel, Verdana, and Calibri work well.

Words per Line The text will be easiest to read if the margins are set to create 10-12 words per line. Margins that are wider or narrower create text that's harder to read.

Justification Left justified text, also called ragged right, is the easiest to read. It doesn't look as nice as full justified, which has a smooth edge on both margins.

Full justified is more fashionable, but it creates uneven spaces between words, which is slightly distracting and takes more effort to read.

Page Layout Whitespace is an important element in the document design. Wide margins and generous space between the chapter title and the beginning of the text make an attractive document.

Chapter Titles Chapter titles are usually written in a san serif font, unlike text in the body of the document which has ornamental serifs.

The chapter number is both smaller and a paler color than the chapter title, in order to draw less attention to it. Both are in an ornamental font different from text in the body of the document.

---

[40] I use Dynamics in Document Design by Karen Schriver, and when I say her methods produced good results, I mean that five people in my critique group copied my formatting and used it in their own books.

Headers are found at the top of the page. Usually the title of the book is on the right, and either the chapter name or the author's name are on the left. Headers are usually omitted on the first page of a chapter.

Headers are typically in the same font as the text in the body of the document, but half a point smaller.

Page Numbers Typically in the same font as the text in the body of the document, but half a point smaller.

Initialen The large ornamental first letter of the chapter is called an Initialen Cap. Eileen Caps, the font used in the example here, is one of the easy to use because it doesn't create an uneven spacing between the first and second lines of text.

This is the first page of a novel. The document design was done by internationally famous document design expert Karen Schriver. [41]

Things to notice about the layout:

- The text is ragged right, the easiest justification to read.
- The text is Book Antiqua, 10.5 points. It was chosen for being easy to read. Times New Roman is also, but not as much.
- Each paragraph is indented five spaces. There is no white space between paragraphs.
- The header and page number are in the same font as the text, but a point smaller.
- The header and page number are in the same font as the text, but a point smaller.
- The chapter number is pale, and in a smaller font than the title.
- There is considerable space between the chapter title and the first line.
- The Initialen capital, the decorative first letter, is Eileen Caps, one of the few that doesn't make a noticeable space between lines.

---

[41] In the interest of full disclosure. I only have access to someone of her caliber because she's a relative.

Chapter 1 The Foundling

rzahil's mother slid out of bed and crawled toward the door until her arms collapsed beneath her. She lay on the floor, and her breath came in wheezing gasps. After a time, she struggled to regain her hands and knees, but fell again, and lay still.

Urzahil abandoned the warmth of the blankets and toddled over to her. He clung to her all night, waiting for her to wake up while her body cooled in his arms. By the time the horizon lightened to grey, he was desperately hungry and needed to nurse. He began to cry.

After a time, the door opened and filled the room with light. Urzahil looked up. The woman from next door stood in the doorway, her hand over her mouth, her eyes wide. Urzahil clung to his mother even more tightly, the woman had to pry his fingers loose before she could pull him to his feet and lead him outside.

That evening, Urzahil sat at the big farm table in the neighbor's kitchen, his feet dangling over the hard-packed dirt floor. The room smelled of smoke. A few coals burned on the hearth, enough to warm the room and drive off the chill of the ocean fogs that blanketed the city in winter.

Urzahil pushed pieces of bread around the plate that had been placed in front of him. The murmur of women's voices flowed over him, the chitchat of the neighbor ladies from up and down the street. He caught a number of words that were familiar to him, but he couldn't put together their meaning.

"My husband went to her village and talked to her people there, but they don't want him. They disowned her when her

A page formatted with chapter title and Initialen

Strategies for Pantsers

"When the hobbits arrived in Bree, they didn't know who Strider was. I didn't know either."

J.R.R. Tolkien

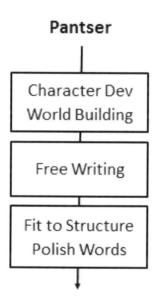

Pantsers dive in without planning and write by the seat of their pants. They get their best ideas during free-writing, and often experience writing as a process of discovery. Their stories are typically character-driven.

Pantsers Are Different

*"If the two of you are exactly alike,
one of you isn't necessary."*

An observation about marriage

Planners and Pantsers are Different

Planning-strategy (Planner) and revision-strategy (Seat-of-the-Pantser) are the two most widely recognized writing techniques. [42] Researcher David Galbraith (1994) was the first to study them separately.[43]

Galbraith gave university students a personality test, the Snyder (2009) self-monitoring index. [44] A high score is associated with modifying one's behavior to achieve a desired effect in social situations, a low score with someone who's more impulsive or exuberant.

Galbraith theorized that high scores were associated with high levels of planning and low scores with spontaneous writing. He divided the group into thirds and called the upper and lower ones planning-strategy and revision-strategy, respectively. Revision-strategy is so named because free-written text takes more cycles of revision than does text that was planned ahead of time.

---

[42] Marleen Kieft, Gurt Rijlaarsdam, and Hull van den Bergh, *"The effect of adapting a writing course to students' writing strategies"*, British Journal of Educational Psychology, 2007
[43] David Galbraith and Mark, Torrance *"The writing strategies of graduate research students in the social sciences* , Higher Education pg. 379-392, 1994
[44] Mark Snyder and Steve Gangestad, *"On the nature of self-monitoring"*, Journal of Personality and Social Psychology" 51, pg. 125-139, 1986

Planner and Pantser Quality, Speed Is the Same

Mark Torrance (1999) did an experiment in which he asked undergraduates to record their writing processes while they wrote school essays. He used their grades to measure quality and estimated efficiency, or writing speed, from the logs the students kept.

Torrance found no evidence that it outperformed revision-strategy, either in quality or speed.[45]

Don't Try To Change Your Type

Marleen Kieft (2007) did an experiment in which high school students, divided into planning-strategy and revision-strategy writers, were given additional instruction in either planning or revision techniques. She found that planning-strategy writers benefited most from planning training, while revision-strategy benefited most from revision training. Furthermore, revision-strategy writers, whose writing was equal to planning-strategy writers, saw their writing quality go down when they used the strategies of planners.

The irony is that high-school teachers often encourage revision-strategy writers to use the methods of planners, to outline and to plan what to say before writing. Pantsers should ignore this advice, as it makes writing less fun and hurts the quality of their work.

Dual Strategies

Based on what we know, planning-strategy should be more efficient and produce better results than writing without planning and patching it up afterwards.

---

[45] Mark Torrance, Glyn Thomas, and Elizabeth Robinson, *"Individual differences in the writing behaviour of undergraduate student"*, British Journal of Educational Psychology, pg. 189-199, 1999

David Galbraith (2009) resolved the apparent contradiction by suggesting dual processes operate in parallel, the familiar outlining strategy, but also a more mysterious free writing strategy that's mostly hidden, and harder to observe. [46]

Strategy 1 - Outlining

The outlining strategy allows the writer to separate the process of developing new ideas from the process of putting them into words.

Bereiter and Scardamalia (1987) observed that idea generation and the generation of text are both high-level functions, either one of which could use most of the writer's cognitive resources and short-term memory.
Separating the two processes prevents them from interfering with each other, and results in better quality writing.

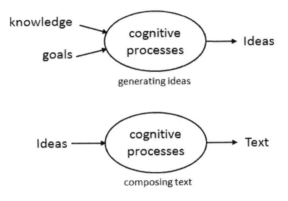

Separate the two high-level processes

Ron Kellogg (1988) agreed with this model, and presented compelling evidence that outlining produced more successful text.

If you're a Planner, outlining is probably the most creative phase of the writing process, and the one you enjoy the most. Ideas come thick and

---

[46] David Galbraith, *"Writing as Discovery"*, British Journal of Educational Psychology, 2009

fast, and you work out almost all the details of your story before you ever put pen to paper.

It's also likely that many of your ideas come to you in non-verbal form. Nonverbal thinking is very common, it's possible that much of our thought takes a form other than words.

> *I was trying to describe a postern door in the main gate of a castle. A postern door admits one man at a time, and is designed to make him defenseless while he's doing it. He has to step over a knee-high threshold while crouching beneath a lintel no higher than his shoulders, and it's so narrow he can't use his arms.*
>
> *I've climbed through the posterns in a number of castles and forts. I had a clear mental image of what they looked like and how it felt to squeeze through them. It would take me about ten seconds to draw one, a little rectangle in a big wooden gate, yet after working on a description for an hour, I still didn't feel that I'd nailed it.*
>
> *While the image of the gate was vivid and sharply detailed, it wasn't a verbal thought, and I was having a hard time translating it into words.*

If your ideas are nonverbal, you may find it easier to develop them in a nonverbal realm with visual tools like diagrams, sketches, or timelines. The thoughts that are verbal probably come to you as sentence fragments, more easily put in an outline than expressed as well-formed prose.

Nonverbal Tools used by Planners:
- o Outlines
- o Concept maps (alternative to outlines)
- o Mountain range plot (major plot points of the Three Act Play)
- o Decision trees (turning points)
- o Timelines/Pert charts
- o Social networks
- o Maps
- o Schematics
- o Assembly instruction (pictures only)
- o Storyboards

Outlining isn't the only nonverbal tool for working on ideas. Maps, timelines, or diagrams with circles and arrows are all useful for pinning down concepts before they're translated into words.

Strategy 2 – Free Writing

Peter Elbow (1973) observed that free writing, the production of text without planning beforehand, was a rich source of new ideas, and that the first spontaneous draft was the richest of all.[47]

Not only that, but free writing seems to produce more of the high-quality writing Bereiter and Scardamalia (1987) called knowledge-transforming. Unlike knowledge-telling, a form of "read and recite", knowledge-transforming writing occurs when the author reflects upon what he knows and adds his own unique insights.

knowledge-telling	Tell what you know.
knowledge-transforming	Reflect on what you know, then make it your own.

knowledge-telling vs. knowledge-transforming

This should have not have been possible under the 'separate to processes' model. David Galbraith (2006) set out to resolve the apparent contradiction.

He wondered if, in addition to outlining, there was a second process operating at the same time, in the background and mostly hidden. It might have to do with the way semantic memory, which stores concepts and symbols, is accessed.

Semantic memory isn't organized sequentially, it's more like a junk drawer in your head. You might find what you're looking for easily enough, but you'll also pull out whatever happened to be next to it.

---

[47] Peter Elbow, *"Writing without Teachers "*, Oxford University Press, 1973

If Stephen King were an outliner writing a story about puberty, he'd include things like middle school, acne, puppy love, and so on. But he isn't an outliner, he's well known to be a Pantser. According to himself, when he reached into Semantic memory for puberty, he also came up with telekinesis.[48]

Visual, Verbal, and Kinesthetic

People vary in the way they like to receive information. Someone may reveal their type through their choice of words, "I see what you mean." or "Yeah, I hear you". I say "It was the best concert I ever saw" then realize I just described something auditory in visual words.

Visual	receive information through their eyes. They like to read and can interpret charts and graphs easily. They like to take notes and draw.
Auditory	receive information through their ears, and retain more from lectures than books. They enjoy conversation and music, and like to ask and answer questions.
Kinesthetic	receive information through feeling or touch, colors, sounds, and scent. They like to get up and move. They remember best when they learn by doing.

Three ways to receive information

Based on no actual data, I wonder if Planners are mostly visual learners and Pantsers are mostly auditory.

---

[48] Stephen King, "On Writing" and "Carrie"

After writing the list of outline-like tools, meaning tools that enabled Planners to do high-level planning without having to compose text, I noticed that every one of those tools was based on drawings, plots, or charts. On the other hand, Pantsers appear to put their thoughts into words with ease when they're free writing. Perhaps their thoughts originate as words, and don't need to be translated.

If most Planners were visual learners whose thoughts were first formed as visual images, it would explain why outlining, and nonverbal techniques in general, were easier for them to use. And if most Pantsers were auditory learners, and if their thoughts originated in spoken form, it would explain why it was easy for them to generate ideas and write them down at the same time.

Visual -> Outliner -> Planner
Auditory -> Free Writing -> Pantser

Theory – Planners are visual, Panters are auditory

Preliminary investigations are inconclusive. The most aggressive Pantser I know is a graphic artist. The other ten or so I've pinged are evenly divided between Planners and Pantsers, and as far as I can tell, all of them are kinesthetic. [49]

Hybrid Strategies

'Planner' and 'Pantser' are hypothetical types, the extremes of a continuum. In practice, most writers fall somewhere in between and use techniques from both strategies. They plan more than a pure Pantser, but they do more revision than the one or two drafts of a pure Planner.

I'm mixed type. I enjoy writing outlines, I like list-making in general. But when I start to write, I don't remember to look at my outline, and after I start to write, I think up so much new material that my finished story bears only a superficial resemblance to my original outline.

---

[49] Maier's Law, *"Facts that do not conform to the theory must be disposed of."*

My Own Survey

When my writing speed fell below 270 words a day, I started to think about the traits that separate slow writers from fast.

I already knew expertise slows you down, and that skilled craftsmanship takes time. I wasn't interested in comparing someone drafting narrative exposition to someone crafting fluent prose. Show will always be slower than Tell, and new writers write faster than experienced ones.

But even within a group of writers who are equally skilled, some are faster than others. I thought I knew why. Anyone can tell you outlining is the secret to writing fast. Therefore, Planners will be faster than Pantsers.

But what other traits were important for writing fast? , I needed to learn a little more about how real writers write. As the child of a psychology professor[50] and the subject of countless experiments, I saw nothing strange in following my writing friends around with a clipboard, conducting interviews and administering surveys. Fortunately, they were good natured and put up with me until my attention wandered off onto some other project.

I surveyed members from all three of my writing critique groups, a total of twenty-six people. I wanted to find out, what are the traits of a fast writer, and what writing strategies do they use? To find out, I surveyed the members of three writing critique groups, a total of twenty-six people.

Survey Questionnaire: Part I - Traits

The first part asked participants to indicate where they fell on an axis representing a trait. The second part asked them to check off anything they used regularly from a list of common tools and techniques.

---

[50] When I was about five, my father took me to work with him. I remember a large space full of cardboard pigeon boxes with these clever corn feeders you could open and shut, which I later learned belonged to B.F. Skinner.

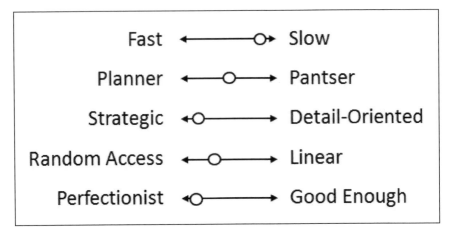

Traits that might affect writing speed

The first part of the questionnaire asked writers to rate themselves on a series of traits by putting a mark on a slider bar between two extremes. (The example above shows my own responses.)

Strategic means starting with the big picture and work to find her and finer levels of detail. The majority of Planners are strategic thinkers, but not all. And occasionally, you find a Pantser who's a strategic thinker.

Linear refers to starting at the beginning of the story and working through to the end, while random access means working in no particular order. Most Pantsers are linear, they start at the beginning and work through to the end. Furthermore, about half of all Planners assemble their outlines in a random access manner, adding detail to the end, beginning, and middle as the ideas strike them.

Perfectionism is found in writers of all writing styles, and it's always associated with slow writing.

I fall halfway between Planner and Pantser, which means I have a foot in each camp, and use some of the techniques from each. I'm a perfectionist, and I write very slowly.

Survey Questionnaire: Part II - Tools and Methods

Planning - Tools and Methods
- Outline
- Three Act Play
- Hero's Journey
- Storylines
- Scene Lists
- Treatments
- A short Synopsis
- Beat Sheets
- Storyboards
- Character Development
- World Building
- Scene Plans

Drafting - Tools and Methods
- Narrative Exposition (Tell)
- Give Self Permission to Write Badly
- Add Reader Emotional Experience (Show not Tell, etc.)
- Wording (Fluency)
- Free Writing
- Start from a Writing Prompt
- Compose while Editing
- Copy editing during Drafting

Revision - Tools and Methods
- Top-Down Revision
- Revision Plan
- Edit Structure
- Edit Content
- Revise Structure and Surface at Same Time
- Add Reader Emotional Experience (Show not Tell, etc.)
- Wording (Fluency)
- How Many Edit Cycles?
- Copy edit during Revision

Tools and Methods for the three phases of writing

The second part of the survey asked writers to check the tools and methods they used regularly. Separate lists were given for each major phase of writing, Planning, Drafting, and Revision.

I expected Planners and Pantsers to use the planning tools differently, with Planners using them before they began to write, and Pantsers during revision. I also expected Planners to favor the Three Act Play, and Pantsers the Hero's Journey. Surprisingly, Planners used both of them, while the Pantsers said they didn't use either.

Survey Results

When the survey results came back, my eyes bulged on stalks. The survey revealed that Pantsers write as fast as Planners. There's no speed advantage to being a Planner. None. [51]

My first thought was to burn the data and never let it see the light of day. The survey results turned my theory on its head and wrecked the premise for this book. But I come from a scientific family where data-burning is frowned upon, and I still wanted to be allowed home for Thanksgiving, so it wasn't a good option.

The data survived, and I was forced to address the question, how can Pantsers write as fast as Planners if they don't plan before writing?

It turns out that everyone plans, but not everyone plans in the same way.

Planner planning tends to be plot-driven, while Pantser planning is mostly about character development and world building. Planners make outlines, map plot points to beat sheets, and draw on huge sheets of butcher paper. Pantsers have long conversations with their characters, identify turning points that will force them to change, and think about the world in which their characters live.

---

[51] At the time, I wasn't familiar with Torrance's work on undergraduate essay writing strategies. (1999) In fact, I wasn't familiar with writing research at all. If I'd bothered to read the seminal papers *before* launching into this project, I wouldn't have condicted investigations and 'discovered' things that were already known.

Pantsers do much of their planning in their heads. But even though it's not visible, it's still planning.

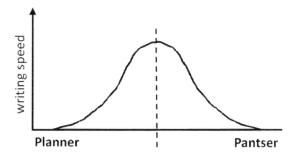

The second surprise was that the slowest writers come from the extreme ends of the continuum, Planners who work from a fifty-page outline and Pantsers who start from nothing but a writing prompt. The fastest writers can be found in the middle. They may lean towards being a Planner or Pantser, but can use the methods of either, depending on the task or their mood.

Most sources say that two thirds of writers are Planners and one third or Pantsers. In my survey, it was more like half-and-half. The survey also asked writers for their Meyers-Briggs type. It turns out that virtually all writers, 90% or more, are introverts.

Traits of a Fast Writer

What distinguishes a fast writer from a slow one? These are the results of the survey.

Things that speed you up:

Planning can take a number of forms, either written down or in your head. It can involve things of your own inventions, or borrowed structures like the conventions of a genre. The line between planning and drafting is not well defined, free writing is a form of planning. But whatever kind of planning you do, a plan will make the rest of the writing process go faster.

Fast Drafting The fastest writers draft in narrative exposition, without editing. The slowest writers both polish their wording and copy edit while composing.

Revise High to Low   Revise the structure before trying to fix the wording. Editing while composing seems to produce less fluent text. It's also said to be one of the major causes of writer's block. Trying to do all levels of revision at the same time, structural, wording, and line editing, not only causes you to throw away text into which you've put significant effort, it also causes you to leave one task unfinished because you get distracted by something else.

Be a Good Reader   Having a head full of memorized phrases will make it easier to compose well-formed text.

Write Every Day   When you've the various writing strategies, they become second nature and are more immediately accessible to you. When the craft is second nature, you have more thought available for composing text.

Things that slow you down:

Perfectionism   slows you down, but doesn't seem to convey any benefits. In fact, it will probably reduce the quality of your writing. Perfectionism in writing takes many forms: doing structural and surface revision together, copy editing and formatting too early, and trying to edit and compose at the same time. Editing while composing is one of the worst things you can do. It seems to produce less fluent text, and it's also said to be one of the chief causes of writer's block.

Strategies for Planners and Pantsers

If both Planners and Pantsers plan, then both of them can do PDR. However, the way they do PDR is very different. Pantsers are often detail-oriented, so it's hard for them to plan at the story level.

Example – Deer in the headlights

I once asked a friend who's an extreme Pantser, "Tell me in once sentence what your story is about." Her eyes widened like a deer caught in the halogens the moment before impact. Just because a sentence is short doesn't mean it's easy.

For a top-down Planner, a one sentence storyline is second nature, but for a detail-oriented Pantser, it can be inaccessible. On the other hand, Pantsers are said to be more creative and better at character development. Each writing strategy has its own strengths and is done in its own way.

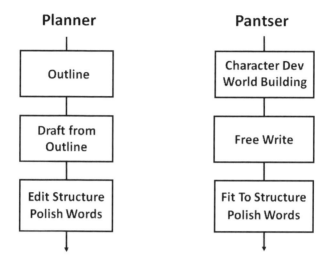

PDR for Planners and Pantsers

Planners   Write an outline and draft it in narrative exposition. Revise the structure using tools like beat sheets or timelines. When the structure has the shape you want, polish the wording.

Pantsers   Plan in your head, mostly about character development and world building. You could begin with a writing prompt and then free write, one of the richest sources of new ideas. Drape the text over a standard framework like the Three Act Play or the Hero's Journey, then polish the wording.

Even though the two approaches are different, they're both PDR. The one that's most comfortable will work best. And whichever version you use, it will help you to write faster.

Stories In Your Head

Writers are more similar than different, no matter what their type. One thing we all seem to have in common is that all of us have stories in our heads.

Example – Downton Abbey

The day after Downton Abbey aired the episode in which Mr. Green assaulted Anna, the lady's maid, I got a note from my sister, "Write a fanfic about Downton Abbey."

"That's not my fandom," I wrote back, but then it occurred to me, I could just jot down the story that had been in my head when I woke up that morning. I penned a short scene, about three pages in length, and sent it to her. [52]

"You have stories in your head?" She sounded surprised.

"You don't?" I asked, equally surprised.

I could remember being about two years old, standing in my crib and composing stories about animals.

"Don't you ever give a movie a different ending or fill in the gaps for a TV show?" No, she didn't.

I asked my other sister. She also said no. That wasn't what I expect to hear. Both sisters are creative. One had gone to art school, and the other took creative writing classes.

I asked my dad if he had stories in his head, and he said yes. That made sense, when we were small, he told fantastical stories about our future selves having fabulous adventures in an imaginary jungle. There was one in which we escaped from a gigantic python by feeding it the rotten food from our backpacks.

All three of my kids, elementary school students, have stories in their heads. My young daughter writes hers in a composition notebook. I was so proud! Until I read her stories and realized she's killed more people than Cecil B. DeMille.

I asked people at work if they had stories in their heads. I made it clear that by 'story' I didn't mean anything sophisticated, just something like a daydream about characters in a book. Some did and some didn't, in about equal numbers. But when I asked people in my writing group, it was 100%. It seemed as though all writers have stories of their heads.

---

[52] published as "A Police Matter" on www.fanfiction.net

Pantser Planning

"There are three rules for writing a novel.
Unfortunately, no one knows what they are."

Somerset Maugham

Pantsers plan, but much of their planning is done in their head. Pantser planning takes the form of character development and world building.

Pantsers usually have a sense of how the story begins and ends, even if they don't yet know much about the middle, and the structure may be shaped to a large extent by the conventions of the genre.

A Pantser may be comfortable jotting down a few bullets for a scene, but not a whole story.

Everybody Plans

Calling a writer who works from an outline a Planner is misleading, because everybody plans. There are writers create multipage outlines, stacks of index cards, and elaborate charts on butcher paper before they put down a single word. Their stories tend to be plot-driven, with events arranged in chronological order. Others don't write down a plan before they start, they plan in their heads.

If they are working within a particular genre, the conventions of the genre provide structure. If the genre is Science Fiction, there will be high technology and aliens. If it's Romance, the girl and the boy will be together at the end. If it's High Fantasy, good will battle evil and good will prevail in the end, unless you're George R.R. Martin.[53]

Stories written by Seat-of-the-Pantsers tend to be character driven, and long before they pick up a pen, they come to know their characters well. They know what their characters want, who their friends and adversaries are, the food they eat and the style of clothing they wear. Even if it's not visible to others, it's still planning.

---

[53] "Why isn't George R.R. Martin allowed on Twitter? Because he killed all 140 characters."

Character Development

*"Every character should want something,
even if it is only a glass of water."*

Kurt Vonnegut

What the Character Wants

The most important part of character development is understanding
what the character wants. The character's needs include things like the
need to belong, the need to be admired, or the need for his job to still be
there the next day. The character himself might be unaware of his
needs, or may not understand the extent to which he's driven by them.

Maslow's Hierarchy of Needs

To get a sense of human needs and their relative importance to each
other, consider Maslow's Hierarchy of needs.[54]

Self-Actualization   also called realizing one's full potential, it
refers to the need for creative expression, the pursuit of
knowledge, spirituality, and a sense of meaning. A craftsman
seeks artistic freedom for self-actualization, so does someone on
a spiritual quest.

---

[54] Hierarchy of needs proposed by Abraham Maslow in his 1943 paper, "*A
Theory of Human Motivation*".

110

Respect The need to be held in high regard by others. One character might seek to win the admiration of others through professional achievement, another might attempt to feel worthy by striving to be a good person.

Belonging The need to be included in a group, the need for friends, the need to be loved. Someone in a new place far from home would long for company, a disowned family member might long for somewhere to go on the holidays.

Safety The need for security, either physical, financial, or emotional. A character who'd been laid off repeatedly might want a full-time salaried position because the insecurity threatened his sense of safety. A character in a home with domestic violence would have a great need for calm and predictability.

Survival The need for air, water, food, sleep, warmth, and safety. A homeless character on a freezing night would need a warm place to sleep, a soldier on the battlefield might need a rock behind which to take cover.

Virtually all character needs can be found somewhere in this pyramid. The most basic needs must be satisfied before the need higher up in the pyramid.

Someone who can't breathe (survival) isn't thinking about starvation (survival, but not as urgent), and someone who's ducking gunfire (survival) isn't concerned about an eviction notice (safety).

There's more flexibility in the upper levels, for example, a person can be unemployed (safety) can still interested in creating art (self-actualization).

Fractal Decomposition for Character Development

I started thinking about using fractal decomposition for character development. It seemed to me that one would develop the character's personality first, with enough backstory to explain it, for example, create a villain who'd been abused as a child.

I ran it by the Pantsers in my critique group. They were quick to tell me I had it all wrong.

Pantsers are skilled at character development and know a lot of techniques. They said that when you develop a character, the first thing you need to know is, "What does the character want?" The second thing is, "Why does he want it?" which usually means understanding key events in the character's past.

Then you need to consider the character's role in the story: hero, mentor, friend, love interest, antagonist, minion, foil, or comic relief. A character's role can change as the story unfolds, a minor character can become more important, a love interest might later betray the hero, but every character in the story has a role.

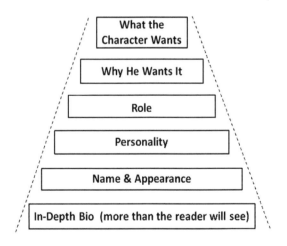

Fractal Decomposition for Character Development

Only after a character's motive and role are established is his personality developed. The character's name and appearance are almost incidental, and are chosen late in the process.

If the character is important, you may want to continue filling out his dossier, much in the way that sales people do for their most important clients. "Is he left or right handed?" "What are his interests?" "Does he have children, and if so, what are their names?" You'll end up with more information than the reader will ever see, but it's normal not to use everything you have. It will still give your writing more depth.

Character development should be done for main characters and antagonists both, and for all major supporting characters.

Character Development Tools

These are some useful tools for character development.

Photo of Character Photos from catalogs and magazines, stills from movies in your genre, and drawings on sites like Pinterest and DeviantArt are particularly good places to find images that can tell you more about your character.
   Displaying the image of your character where you can see it easily is a useful writing technique.

Character Cards Character cards are like baseball cards, with a picture of the character, their name, their role in the story, and a sentence or two of backstory or motive. There's fun to make, and illustrate the character development so far.

Character Dossiers Some pantsers recommend developing the character's biography in great detail. These contain extensive backstory, including traumatic events or emotional wounds that occurred in childhood. If the bio is long enough, the level of detail may be far more than the reader will ever see.

Composites of Real People Ideas come from somewhere. It's unlikely that you'd lift a whole person, but you might use a turn of phrase from one, something that happened to another, and some aspect of the physical appearance of a third.

People don't usually recognize themselves in print, anyway. My sister looked up from one of my stories and said, "This scene where he gets seasick. The oily roll of the waves, the smell of fish in the bilge, you got it just exactly right." I decided not to say, "Umm, that was you."

Conversely, one real person may be divided into pieces and find their jokes, mannerisms, various aspects of their appearance, clothes, life experiences, and walk distributed among half a dozen different characters. Creative people may be original, but they still get their ideas from somewhere.

Music / Playlists To generate a mood to evoke a particular sort of person.

Method Acting A technique used by actors to summon up the thoughts and feelings of their characters to create a more realistic performance. A method actor can cry real tears on demand, or make a vein throb with anger.

Method acting is also used by writers to good effect, particularly those who write Deep POV. By experiencing the thoughts and feelings of their characters, they're more able to describe what their characters are going through.

Character Interviews

If you get stuck, it helps to sit your character down and interview them. Ask them what they saw, how they felt about it, what they wanted to do. Don't limit yourself to main characters.

Some people like to figure out who their characters are by sitting them down and interviewing them. This can be especially helpful with a minor character you don't know well, particularly a villain. Ask them, "Why did you do what you just did?" or "Did that conflict remind you of something in your past? An old wound from your backstory, perhaps?"

To help with the interviews, you can find lists of interview questions online. Some people love them, and some hate them. I think it has to do with what questions they expect to see, "What does your character take in his coffee?" is feeble compared to, "Is your character living a lie?"

Here are a few questions that should bring out interesting things about your characters.

Character interview questions:

What do you want? That's fine, but what do you *really* want?
- What makes you laugh out loud?
- What to do when you're angry?
- What things do you *not* like to do?
- Is there anything you've always wanted to do but haven't? What would happen if you did it?
- What's a strong memory that has stuck with you since childhood? Why is it so powerful and enduring?
- Have you ever been in love? Had a broken heart?
- What you most ashamed of in your life?
- What's the worst thing you could do to other character?
- What's the worst thing other character could do to you? What you deserve it?
- What do you pretend to be? What's behind the mask?

Decision Trees

Turning points are decisions, so they can be mapped in the form of a decision tree, initially developed as a business tool.

Decision trees take the form of forks in the road, which lead to other forks, and so on. Any given path through the decision tree can be a character arc, and the decisions along it are the turning points that define the character arc.

You can map out a series of possible decisions when planning your story, or more likely, jot down the decisions as they come up. You might go down one path, backtrack, and pursue some other direction instead.

Example - The Bounty Mutiny

The decision tree represents the choices available to Fletcher Christian during the voyage of the HMS Bounty in 1789.

The Bounty mutiny is unique in British naval history. In most mutinies, the captain and officers were killed and thrown overboard and the mutineers, illiterate sailors, left no written records of the event.

In the Bounty mutiny, no one died, and people on both sides left detailed accounts.

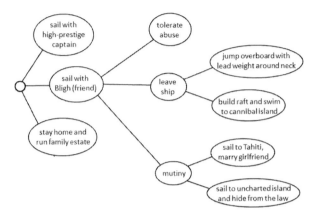

Mapping turning points with a decision tree

The turning points, the decisions made by first officer Fletcher Christian, are the key elements of the story structure.

Fletcher Christian hero-worshiped Captain William Bligh, his friend and mentor, the greatest navigator of the day. On their first voyage together, Christian was so keen on sailing with Bligh that, when there were no officer positions available, he sailed before the mast.

When the HMS Bounty went to Tahiti to collect breadfruit, Bligh handpicked his own crew and he chose Christian as one of his officers. Bligh openly favored Christian, and before long, promoted him to second-in-command over a more senior officer.

They reached Tahiti. During a long layover, most of the men, including Christian, formed attachments with Polynesian women.

Bligh, who was well-intentioned but had poor social skills, would fly into a rage and belittle people around him. No one was exempt, but Christian got the worst of it. On one occasion, Bligh cursed him and threatened to have turned before the mast and flogged. Christian took it hard, and came to believe he wouldn't survive the voyage.

Bligh was unaware of the effect he had on others. He lost his temper, he yelled, and he felt better. That's just the way he was. It never would have occurred to him to apologize.

On April 28, 1789, Christian gave away all his possessions and asked a friend to tell his mother he loved her. Then he built a small raft, intending to slip over the side during the night. He was a strong swimmer and thought he could reach a nearby island. The island was later found to be inhabited by cannibals, so it wasn't the best idea he'd ever had.

That evening when he came on deck, the ship was crowded with sailors watching a volcano erupt. Orange light reflected from the water, dozens of people were looking at it. He had no chance of slipping away unseen. Then someone spotted a shark and called to the bosun to open the arms chest so he could shoot it.

Christian followed them and took a pistol from the arms chest. He held it in his hand, thinking. The men watched him. Christian was a popular officer. Whatever he decided to do, they would follow him.

One might expect a decision tree to take the form, "At a fork in the road, choose a path, proceed to the next fork, choose another path" always going forward.

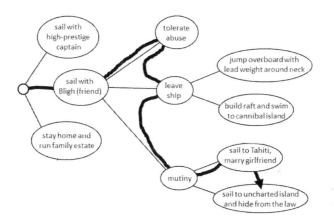

Turning Points – The decisions Christian actually made

The diagram of a real person's real decisions is not that clean. Christian chose a path, backtracked, chose an earlier, less-favored option, rejected that too, then took the only option remaining.

Note that a decision tree only shows decisions made by the character, it does not show events. Christian died by being axe-murdered, and while that was an important event in the story, at least to him, it wasn't a turning point of the story. Turning points are decisions, and being murdered wasn't a decision on his part.

World Building

*"A blank piece of paper is God's way of telling
us how hard it is to be God."*

Sidney Sheldon

One of the special aspects of both Science Fiction and Fantasy writing is world building.

Worldbuilding can a massive task which includes inventing a new geography, political system, social order, and culture. Supporting these are the hundreds of details about agriculture, trade, currency, music, language, art, and food.

Aspects of world-building to consider:

Geography and Terrain	Trade
Place Names	Law
Political Systems	Social Systems
Agriculture	Professions
Commerce	Medicine
Currency	Social customs
Weapons and Warfare	Cuisine
Armies	Clothing styles
Horsemanship	How the local economy works
Seamanship	Plants and animals
Fortifications	Weather patterns and Climate
Rules Of Magic	Religion
Language	Alien Cultures

What clothing do people wear? At court, on an ordinary day, for a festival? What do they eat for supper, at a banquet, on a high holy day? How do most people earn their living? How would they treat a broken leg, or an infection? What do they fear most, war, crop failures, or their neighbors?

World Building in Historical Fiction

Writers of historical fiction also do world building. Their worlds are real times and places, which means for the most part, they're researched rather than invented.

However, the details of a historical setting aren't necessarily known to modern scholarship, leaving the writer to either invent them or fill in the blanks using other sources.

World Building in Fantasy

Many Fantasy worlds are based on Medieval Europe. Fantasy stories often include a hierarchical society with a lord and nobles at the top, and have lots of castles, sword fights, and horses.

Having majored in medieval history for a time, I was struck by how much Christianity dominated the thoughts of medieval people. It made its way into everything from the calendar ("On St. Crispen's day, an hour after terce") to swear words. ("by Saint Loy!" or the much stronger, "God's wounds!")

Yet in Fantasy writing, mention of Christianity as it was practiced in medieval Europe is almost nonexistent, while magic, which medieval people did not have, is widespread. This may be because in Tolkien's "*Lord of the Rings*", the epic which defined the High Fantasy genre and established most of its tropes, any mention of Christianity was absent.[55] The only formal religion in his world was practiced by characters on the evil side. [56]

On the other hand, Tolkien gave his characters an abundance of magical abilities: they could kindle fires, foretell the future, become invisible, shape-shift, call up storms, or perform necromancy. Real medieval people wouldn't have tolerated people who used magic. ("*She's a witch, burn her!*") Fantasy tropes still follow the conventions

---

[55] This is surprising because Tolkien was a deeply religious person.
[56] The Cult of Melkor, which a) is fake, and b) involves human sacrifice. These were not good people.

Tolkien established, with less religion and more magic than would have been found in medieval Europe.

Of course, Fantasy worlds don't have to be European. Other worlds have been built on the Chinese or Japanese medieval period. And Star Wars, a work of Fantasy rather than Science Fiction, is set in space with worlds built on a dozen planets.

Even though your world will be different than a real historical setting, do pay attention to how real societies work. Your world doesn't have to be real, but it does need to have verisimilitude, which means that while it's not real, it could be.

In writing group, someone submitted a story in which the entire economy was based on thieving. It was pointed out that not everyone can be a pickpocket. Someone has to plow the fields, cast the fishing nets, and bake the bread, otherwise they'd all starve.

World Building in Science Fiction

"The good science fiction novel should be able to predict not the automobile but the traffic jam." Frederick Pohl

Science Fiction writers often use earth cultures as a basis for alien civilizations. Native American cultures, Oriental, Aboriginal, Utopian societies, or artificial environment like a submarine or an Antarctic outpost during the winter can all provide material for Science Fiction settings.

Be consistent with the tropes of your genre or sub-genre about which of the laws of physics you can break. Faster-than-light speed travel and time travel is almost universally accepted, but if you violate other laws of physics like conservation of mass, Doppler shift, or photosynthesis, you'll get in trouble. But whatever you choose to follow or break, be consistent.

World Building Resources

Start by reading novels in which world building is done particularly well. For Science Fiction, novels that do world building extremely well include:

- o *Ringworld* by Larry Niven
- o *The Dispossessed* by Ursula Le Guin

For Fantasy, some of the best examples are:

- *The Lord of the Rings* by J.R.R. Tolkien
- *Lord Foul's Bane* by Stephen R. Donaldson
- *The Merovingen Nights* series by C.J. Cherryh

The materials produced for role playing games (RPG) can provide a surprisingly rich resource for world building:

- ICE (Iron Crown Enterprises)
- GURPS (Generic Universal Role Playing System)

Whatever you're looking for, you can probably find it. There's even a GURPS mauals for building underwater worlds.

Don't overlook reference manuals written specifically for for writers. I particularly like *"The Writer's Complete Fantasy Reference"* by Terry Brooks and *"Wizards, Aliens, and Starships: Physics and Math in Fantasy and Science Fiction"* by Charles L. Alder.

Invented Languages

A number of Science Fiction and Fantasy worlds have languages developed for those worlds, not just names for people and places, but whole languages. Both the Star Trek and Star Wars movies featured invented languages developed by professional linguists. J.R.R. Tolkien, a linguist at Oxford University, wrote The Lord of the Rings in large part to give his invented languages a place to live. Some fans are so taken with the languages, they actually learn to speak them. [57]

Building The World First

One of the Pantsers in my writing group, says he does world building before he does any other part of the story, even character development. I thought he was unique in that respect, until recently, when my teenage daughter started designing an underground world in a science fiction setting, independent of characters or plot.

---

[57] I'm in a mixed marriage. I speak Elvish and my husband speaks Klingon.

Story Structure

*"I was supposed to write a romantic comedy, but
my characters broke up."*

Ann Brashares

Unless you're working from a story prompt and are exploring to see where it goes, you probably have a sense of how your story begins and ends, as well as a few major events along the way.

Conventions of the Genre

If you're working within a genre, the conventions of the genre will provide structure to your story.

Romance In a romance novel, boy will meet girl, something will prevent them from getting together, there will be a rival, and the boy and girl will get together in the end.

Mystery In a mystery novel, there will be false leads, and someone may be falsely accused of the crime, but in the end, the mystery will be solved by the POV character.

Science Fiction In a certain genres of science fiction, aliens will threaten the earth, but after a long struggle, will be defeated in the end.

Fantasy If it's High Fantasy, good will battle evil, and good will prevail, unless the author is George R.R. Martin.

If a story structure is familiar to you, you will be able to make use of it even if you don't map out plots ahead of time.

How To Write Faster

Character Arc

The character arc describes how the character changes over the course of the story. Usually the change takes the form of an improvement, a young person coming of age, a self-centered person who begins to care about other people, or a timid person finding inner strength they didn't know they had.

Turning Points

If you're thinking about a formal structure, it's probably in the form of turning points, the decisions in response to events that reveal character.

A turning point changes the direction of the story. It must involve something big, a dilemma and choice affecting the whole story.

Turning points tend to mirror the events of the plot, but because they're in reaction to events, they occur slightly later.

Turning point occur when the character ...

- o Decides to become involved with the story conflict for the first time.
- o Decides to deal with something he'd rather avoid.
- o Re-evaluates how to deal with an obstacle.
- o Has a change of perspective, a new understanding.
- o Learns that everything he once believed was wrong.
- o Has an epiphany.
- o Changes his goal.
- o Changes his approach to the main conflict.
- o Has a crisis of faith or hope.
- o Experiences a disillusionment.

Note that turning points are usually internal, and involve a change in perspective, a disillusionment, or an epiphany.

123

Planning Tools for Pantsers

Hero's Journey A variation on the Three Act Play, emphasizing how the character changes over the course of the story.

Fractal Decomposition What the character wants, role in the story, backstory, significant traumas in past that explain current actions.

Social Network A diagram of circles and arrows that indicates the characters, their relative importance, and the strength and nature of their relationships with each other.

Free Writing Writing without planning beforehand, a form of planning in itself, and is thought to be one of the best ways to generate new ideas.

Synopsis A short summary. This is a planning tool that can be done with free writing.

Concept Map A diagram of circles connected by lines which represent ideas and the relationships between them. An alternative to outlining.

Treatment A short summary of major events of the story, sort of like a spoken version of an outline, sometimes with drawings and maps.

Decision Tree A business tool showing a series of forks in the road, each representing a decision.

Maps Helpful for keeping track of the movements of your characters, and also a vital tool for world building.

Dossier A standardized questionnaire used by salesmen to record a client's traits. It usually includes the client's favorite place to eat, hobbies, the names of his children, etc. Used as a memory prompt to build and maintain (or fake) a personal relationship.

Pantser Drafting

"I didn't kill him, I discovered him dead."

A mystery novelist who
killed a popular character

If you're a Pantser, you'll probably get most of your ideas while writing successive drafts of your story, although the first, spontaneous draft will probably be the richest in new ideas.

Start from a prompt

Pantsers may start free-writing from a prompt, like a phrase. *"In a hole in the ground there lived a hobbit."*[58]

A writing prompt can also be a situation. Here's one published by WritersDigest.com last Thanksgiving.

> *You've been invited to attend a Thanksgiving dinner at a friend's house, but when you walk in you notice there's no turkey and, instead, a giant "Intervention" sign hanging across the mantle. Your friend, who is surrounded by many of your other friends and family, sits you down and explains that you have a problem: you spend too much time writing! Write this scene and how you handle it.*[59]

My cheeks burned when I read that. *I can stop, I can stop anytime I want to. I just don't want to.*

Another approach is to put a character in a situation of conflict and see what he does. One writer who favors the Pantser strategy observed the character can't be developed in the absence of an antagonist. The conflict itself defines the characters. When he begins a new story, he

---

[58] J.R.R. Tolkien doodled on the back page of a student's exam book.
[59] Writers Digest, www.writersdigest.com/prompts/thanksgiving-intervention

throws two characters together in a situation where there's already tension, and then watches them to see what happens.

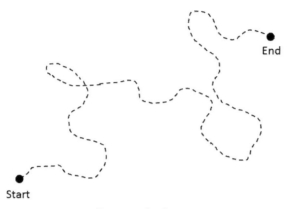

Pantser drafting

Often the writer has a sense of the beginning and end of the story, and maybe some events along the way, but much of the journey is exploring. The Pantser is much more likely than the Planner to be surprised as the story unfolds.

Pantser writing is fun. The story unfolds while it's being written, such that the writer is as surprised as the reader by the things the characters do.

Free writing

Writing is discovery. It's common for writers to say that, but it's actually true. Early research showed that free writing, the writing of successive drafts without planning, is one of the richest sources of new idea generation, and that the early spontaneous first draft is the richest of all.[60]

One difference between novice and expert writers has been described as knowledge-telling vs. knowledge-transforming. [61] Knowledge-

---

[60] Peter Elbow, *"Writing without Teachers "*, Oxford University Press, 1973
[61] Carl Bereiter and Marlene Scardamalia, *"The psychology of written composition"*, 1987

transforming is better, not only because it reflects the author's unique voice, but because knowledge-transformers gain a deeper understanding of their topic.

Knowledge-Telling	Tell what you know
Knowledge-Transforming	Reflect on what you know, and come up with your own take on it

Novice vs. Expert writing styles

Method Acting

A technique used by actors to summon up the thoughts and feelings of their characters to create a more realistic performance. A method actor can cry real tears on demand, or make a vein throb with anger.

Method acting is also used by writers to good effect, particularly those who write Deep POV. By experiencing the thoughts and feelings of their characters, they're more able to describe what their characters are going through.

Music

Many writers listen to music while they're writing. Some have playlists that evoke a character or a setting, Others play stirring pieces to get in the mood to write a battle scene.

While there isn't evidence that Pantsers are auditory learners as a group (although I believe it to be true), more of them seem to write while listening to music.

Pantser Revision

If drafting is about creating your story, revision is about cleaning it up.

When you're free-writing, the story unfolds before you. The plot takes you places you didn't anticipate, and your characters do things that surprise you. At the end of the first draft, you've discovered a great deal about the story that you didn't know when you began.

Pantsers work out what they want to say by writing. Free writing is one of the best ways to get new ideas. Writers say they enjoy being surprised by the turns their plots take and the things the characters do.

Some ideas are better than others, and not everything makes the final cut. Entire scenes or character arcs may end up in the dustbin. Also, exploring makes the story ramble, so there may be some plot excursions that ended up as blind alleys. It's not a problem, it's just the process.

When the first draft is finished, it probably won't have anything even close to a traditional structure. Again, it's not a problem, the structure can be edited into the text after the first draft is finished

Revise Structure

"It's already a home. We're trying to turn it into a house."

Homeowners in the middle
of a renovation

Edit in Structure

Let's say you compose by freewriting, and you've just finished the first draft of your story. Your first task is to shape what you've written into a structure. You must assure yourself you have a complete story with a beginning, middle, and end.

That's the downside of the exuberance and creativity of drafting. At the end of the first draft, your story probably doesn't have a well-defined shape. Your first task in revision is to edit the structure into it.

If Planner structure is like the poles of a tent, an armature waiting to have flesh put on its bones, then Pantser structure is like the tent canvas. There's a lot of material, but it doesn't have a well-defined shape.

To make your story stronger, map it onto a traditional structure. For Pantsers, that means drape your material over a ready-made frame and tug it into shape. It's like hanging a costume on a hanger, it lets you stand back and see what you've got. It won't interfere with your creativity, it's just a tool.

The Three Act Play

Most novels, and virtually all screenplays, are structured according to Aristotle's Three Act Play[62] or its cousin, the Hero's Journey.

---

[62] The alert reader will observe that Aristotle also said that heavy objects fall faster than light objects, but he was right about story structure.

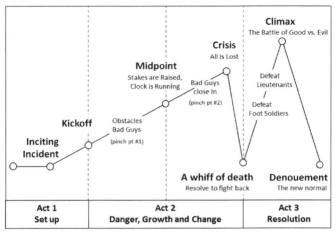

The Three Act Play

The Three Act Play is a part of our culture, or else it's hardwired into our brains, but for some reason, readers seem to find this structure satisfying. If you use it, people will like your story better.

Simplified Version - The Three Disasters

You may prefer to work with a structure called the Three Disasters [63], a simplified version of the Three Act Play developed by Randy Ingermanson.

The Three Disasters captures the major plot points of the three act play, the Kickoff, Midpoint, and Crisis, and place them on the borders between each of the four quarters of the story, which Ingermanson likens to a football field. The Climax goes in the middle of the fourth quarter.

The Three Disasters contains most of the structural information of the Three Act Play, but is easier to use.

---

[63] Randy Ingermanson, *"Writing Fiction for Dummies"*

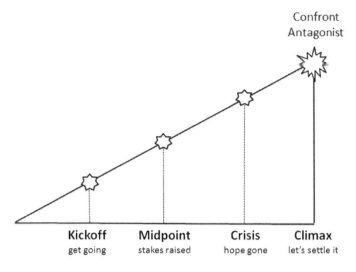

The Three Disasters

Get Going The inciting incident that kicks off the story near the end of the first quarter.

Stakes Raised A point in the middle of the story at which the stakes are raised and the clock starts ticking. This is the point at which the character really commits, and begins to look forward rather than back.

Hope Gone A moment of Despair at the third quarter, from which comes the resolve to confront the enemy.

Climax The final confrontation between good and evil near the end of the story.

These four plot points will be the tie points to map your draft against the structural template. The next step is to find these four points in your story, then map them to a structure.

Why Turning Points Are Important

Blogger Jami Gold says, consider what would happen if any of the parts were missing.

Inciting Incident If the reader doesn't see the inciting incident, they can't know what motivated the character to leave his ordinary life, or understand what he hope to gain by it.
Midpoint This is the point at which the character fully commits to the story conflict, faces his flaw, and starts to change. Without it, you don't have a character arc.

Crisis / Whiff of Death Without the moment when all hope is lost, at least for a moment, the enemy wouldn't seem so dangerous nor the odds so long, and the run-up to the climax would seem like no big deal.

Climax Without a resolution, the story would have no ending. It wouldn't be a story.

If you don't have a Climax or an Inciting Incident, you don't have a beginning and end, which means you don't have a story. If you leave out the Crisis or the Midpoint, you won't have as strong a story as you could have had.

Find the Turning Points in Your Story

Gold suggests asking questions about story events, both plot and character, to determine whether they might be turning points.

How To Identify Turning Points:

o Does the character consider becoming involved with the main story conflict, but hesitate?

o Does the character decide for the first time to become involved with the main story conflict rather than avoid it?

o Does the character except that the main story conflict they then trying to avoid is, in fact, unavoidable in the have to deal with it?

- o Does the character encounter new obstacles or conflicts, complicating his path to the story goal and forcing him to change direction?
- o Does the character see the adversary for the first time?
- o Do the stakes go up significantly?
- o Does the character fully committed himself to the story conflict for the first time, and go from being reactive to proactive?
- o Does the adversary reveal a flaw in the character?
- o Does the character take steps to address the flaw?
- o Does the character form a new goal?
- o Does the character change their approach to the story conflict?
- o Does the character learn everything they'd assumed about the story goal or conflict was wrong?
- o Does the character experience a crisis of faith or hope?
- o Does the character has an epiphany that affects how the proceeds to the story goal?
- o Does the character confront lesser adversaries?
- o Does the character confront the chief adversary and settle everything once and for all?

Even the easier turning points, the Climax, Inciting Incident, and Crisis, aren't always easy to find, even when you know what to look for.

- o They may be in the wrong order.
- o They may occur offstage, or be missing entirely.
- o There may be several plot events, any one of which could plausibly be the turning point you're looking for.

Missing plot points can be written in and order can be switched. Duplicates are a little trickier. One plot point can be made bigger and more intense, and the others toned down. It's also possible to regard multiple plot events as a collection and call the whole group a turning point.

When you revise your own work, you'll have to identify the turning points in your first draft. It might be hard to identify the turning points because they could be out of order, redundant, or missing.

Example – Turning Points in Jurassic Park

Plot points in the movie, Jurassic Park include:

- Paleontologist Alan Grant finds a new dinosaur skeleton.

- A velociraptor kills a park worker / Grant is invited to come to the park to certify its safety.

- Park owner John Hammond's grandchildren join the group. ("stakes raised")

- The tour was disappointing and gave the impression, "Dinosaurs aren't dangerous" ("false victory")

- Grant and the children, stranded in a stalled jeep, are attacked by a T-Rex.

- A lawyer is eaten by a T-Rex while sitting on the toilet.

- Dennis shuts off the security system, gets lost in the storm, and is killed by dinosaurs. ("stakes raised")

- Game warden Muldoon searches for survivors and finds evidence that Grant and the children are alive. ("whiff of death")

- In the Visitor Center kitchen, two velociraptors stalk the children. A T-Rex eats the velociraptors. ("deux ex machina")

- Everyone leaves in a helicopter. Pelicans fly over the waves.

All the turning points are there, and in order. Screenwriters work from a format in which each of turning point is located at a specific place in the movie, so in general, they're easy to find. But even though, like virtually all movies, Jurassic Park followed the standard template, I had trouble identifying some of the major plot points.

The Climax

Identifying the Climax was easy, it usually is. It was the scene in which the two velociraptor stalked the children in the kitchen.

The Climax occurs at the end of the story, when the main character faces the chief adversary and everything is settled once and for all. Often there are a series of lesser clashes leading up to the final confrontation, as minions and then lieutenants attack the hero, but always, it is the battle with the chief villain that defines how the story is resolved.

The Denoument

The Climax is followed by a quiet ramping-down period in which all the loose ends are tied up and the story question is answered if it hasn't been already.

The Kickoff

The Kickoff was harder to identify. It could've been either when Grant accepted the invitation to go to Jurassic Park, but it also could've been earlier when a velociraptor killed a park worker.

The Crisis

The Crisis, often called the "All Hope Is Gone" moment, is often accompanied by a whiff of death. That could have been when Tim was touching the electric fence when the power came back on, but that moment didn't seem as dark as an earlier one, when they were locked out of the security system and the power to the electric fences was down.

The Midpoint

I couldn't find the Midpoint at all. I'd guessed "the stakes are raised" happened when the children arrived and all of a sudden, the danger seemed more important, but that event happened early. I had to go online to learn that the Midpoint occurred when Dennis shut down the electric fences and the dinosaurs got out. The stake raised was, "The park cannot control the dinosaurs."

The Midpoint is the fulcrum of the whole story, when the character realizes this adventure isn't an afternoon in the park, it's a "No $&*%" big deal with terrible consequences for failure. Larry Brooks described it as, "Solving the problem, rather than simply trying to figure out what the problem is before it kills them."[64]

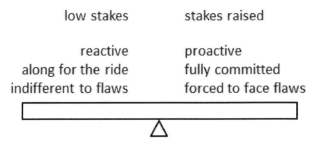

low stakes	stakes raised
reactive	proactive
along for the ride	fully committed
indifferent to flaws	forced to face flaws

The Midpoint is the fulcrum of the story

In spite of its importance, the Midpoint is the hardest point to spot. It shouldn't be, since it's in the exact middle of the story. Look for "the clock starts ticking", a dramatic device that shows the stakes have just been raised. The clock doesn't have to be there, but it's often used to show an increase in tension. If you see it, you've probably found the Midpoint.

If I'd been observant, I'd have noticed that when Dennis left to steal the embryos, he said, "I need eighteen minutes". There was more clock imagery in that scene, a second hand on his computer screen, a cuckoo clock sound in the control room, and a digital clock on the dash of his jeep.

In Titanic, the stakes were raised when the ship was damaged.

"Captain, we've just struck an iceberg."
"How much time do we have?"
"About an hour."

In The Wizard of Oz, the Midpoint occurred when Dorothy was captured.

The witch held up an hourglass filled with blood-red sand.
"Do you see that? That's how much longer you've got to be alive.
And it isn't long, my pretty. It isn't long."

---

[64] Larry Brooks, "Story Engineering" 2011

These are from scripts, and constructed using a fairly exacting formula. It's unlikely you'll find an actual clock at the fulcrum of your story, but you'll probably find a sense of urgency, a speeding up of some sort, at the point where the stakes are raised, and if it's in the middle of the story, then it's probably your Midpoint.

Map Story to Structure Using Tie Points

First, it's important to understand the concept of tie points.

Example – Georectify a Photo to a Map

Tie points were invented to overlay aerial photographs onto maps. In World War I, aircraft flew over the front lines to photograph the trenches. The trench systems were large, and new ones were dug all the time. A pilot wouldn't able to remember what he saw, so they took pictures.

Ideally, the camera was pointed straight down but more often, pictures had to be taken from the side. That distorted the image – things that were close looked bigger than things that were further away, and all the proportions were distorted.

To overlay the aerial photo onto a map, cartographers used tie points. Any physical features in both the photo and the map, like a distinctive building or a crossroads, was used as a tie point.

Once the tie points were matched up, the rest of the photograph (or a sketch of it) was distorted into the shape it would have had, had the camera been aimed straight down.

That's what you want to do with your story, rearrange it shape to match the template without changing its content. It will still be your story, just straightened up a bit.

As in geo-rectification, mapping a story onto a template is done with tie points. For stories, the tie points are the inciting incident, the climax, the crisis, and the midpoint.

Clean Up the First Draft of Free-Writing

After you've mapped the first draft of your story to a structure, it will be much easier to do revisions. Trim the extraneous material generated while exploring and fix the inconsistencies which are a natural consequence of free-writing.

Trim Extra Material that go nowhere. In free-writing, more material is generated than is used, creating blind alleys. Edit them out.

Resolve Contradictions Stories evolve over time, and details may become inconsistent with earlier parts of the story. *In the first Star Wars movie, Luke and Leia share a kiss. Later, the screenwriter realized she was his sister. Eewww!*

Backfill Names Early in the story, the characters visit the tavern where the innkeeper pours their ale. Later in the story, the tavern has become "The Sailor's Rest" and its proprietor, a retired seaman called Allard. You may want to go back and backfill the names, now that you know them.

Backfill Descriptions The first time your characters passed by, they saw a fortified town high in the mountains. With increasing word count, the town became a fortified town behind two sets of walls, accessible only by a narrow footpath under the watch of keen-sighted archers. From the reader's point of view, the detailed description should appear early in the story, not late, when the author invented it.

Use Planning Tools for Revision

As a writer, you can plan structure into your story beforehand, or edit it in afterwards. Either strategy works. Planning tools work just as well for revision as they do for planning.

See What You Have

You've just finished drafting your story. If you're like most Seat-of-the-Pants writers, you're facing a large and disorganized manuscript. In the course of free writing, the story grew and grew. Your ideas changed along the way, so the details aren't always consistent. Some material is redundant, some plot threads wandered off course, there were characters who changed beyond recognition.

Your first task is to look at your story as a whole and see what you have. The trouble is, there's more in a typical story than anyone could keep in their head. That's why writers use planning tools to help them see what they have.

Synopsis Tell yourself the story in a condensed way. What's the story about? What happens in it? How is the main character changed?

Storytelling Tell the story out loud to someone else. Even if they just listen and don't give you any feedback (or in my case, if I'm sitting on someone who's struggling to get away) it's still useful exercise. There's something magical about telling the story aloud that helps clarify what it's about and what you're trying to say.

Outline Jot down a few bullets capturing the major things that happened in the story, and how the characters felt about them.

Treatment A summary of the major events of the story, sometimes with drawings and maps.

Three Act Play A dramatic structure attributed to Aristotle with the plot points inciting incident, midpoint, crisis, climax, and denouement. I like to draw it in the form of the "mountain range" plot, which shows the turning points as peaks and valleys.

Beat sheet A list of the beats in the story, both the major and minor turning points. A beat is any event that forces a decision or reveals character, there may be dozens of beats in a story.

Timeline Show the events of the story shown on a bar graph in the order they happened. Ask:
- o   Was the character in two places at once?
- o   Were two characters in the same place at the same time?
- o   Did the character have knowledge of an event before it happened?

Scene list A list of each scene in the story. Used to make sure action scenes are followed by reaction scenes, and to note the placement of all major plot points in the story.

Scene checklist A list of everything normally included in a scene: purpose, setup, conflicts, and hook. If some of your scenes are missing these elements, the scene checklist will tell you what to fix.

Rearrange the Text

Once you know what you have, rearrange it into the structure of your choice, the Three Act Play, the Hero's Journey, or whatever other structure you want it to have. Move blocks of text around, cut out parts that don't belong, or write new material to fill in what's missing.

I find that what tool I use depends on how much text I'm trying to work on. For something the length of a scene or a short chapter, I use scissors and tape. For something longer, I use index cards to get organized, and Scrivener if I've decided to tear a manuscript apart and rebuild it.

Index Cards A good way to jot down the major ideas and re-arrange them easily.

Butcher Paper Long rolls of paper on which to sketch the events of the story, usually arranged as a timeline. Events or observations may be written on sticky notes and moved around. Most people pin it to the wall or spread it out on the dining room table.

Scissors and Tape I find that when the story gets bigger than I can keep in my head, what works best is to print it out, tape it into one long scroll, then cut it into chunks and lay them out on the dining room table. The downside is that I can't leave the taped-up lengths of paper unwatched, because the cat will eat them.[65]

Ant trails If the story structure won't "jell", rewrite a synopsis over and over until the story threads simplify and fall into place.

Scrivener Import a big block of text into Scrivener, break it into manageable pieces, give them names, move them around like index cards on a corkboard, and view two different parts of the document, no matter how widely separated they are, without having to scroll.

---

[65] Way too much of the children's artwork has suffered this fate.

Revise the Character Arc

Storytelling is about change. Stories are mostly about how a character changed, usually in response to some primal need – to survive, to protect their family, to protect their home, to protect their friends, to save face, to find love, to belong.

In the course of the story, the character goes from being a follower, from being tentative, from being focused on themselves or their immediate circle and circumstances force them to become braver, more resourceful, more far-seeing, to become a leader.

How the Character Could Change:

o   The character grows up and leaves home
o   A timid person finds his courage
o   A materialistic or fame-seeking person becomes more interested in connection with family/community/religion
o   Someone is hardened by traumatic experience and becomes isolated from others
o   Someone lightens up and becomes more tolerant
o   Someone is corrupted by power
o   Someone comes to terms with a terrible loss
o   An abuse spouse leaves and becomes independent
o   Someone faces his deepest fear and finds it's not so terrible
o   Someone stops defining himself in terms of others and finds his own voice

---

The new strengths are forged in suffering and danger and loss, and the character may not even know what he's made of until he's tested. If your character doesn't change or doesn't change enough or in a significant way, strengthen your character arc.

Strengthen the Character Arc

Go up against a more fearsome villain To make the hero braver, smarter, more resourceful, etc., the villain has to be that much more formidable. Give him more strength, make him more resilient, make his motive more compelling, and it will be reflected in the hero.

Make the conflicts and obstacles worse You could have them come from an unexpected source. Instead of being due to adversarial forces, they could come from a crisis of self-confidence or betrayal by friends.

Move the starting point back The hero may be pretty much where he needs to be at the start of the story. If you begin with a hero is too perfect, he has nowhere to go.

If he's already considerate/empathetic/helpful and that's how you want him to be at the end of the story, take some of it away from him.

The Hero's Journey

The Hero's Journey, which defines a character arc, is a useful structure for character-driven stories, which most Pantser stories are. Storytelling is about change. It's usually about growth, but it doesn't have to be, the character could change for the worse.

In some cases, the character doesn't necessarily change over the course of the story, what changes is our understanding of him. This can be particularly true for villains. The villain doesn't grow, but our understanding of his motives might change to the point that we see him differently.

Revise Scene Structure

"No surprise to the writer, no surprise to the reader."

Robert Frost

A scene is a portion of the story which occurs in a single time and place, and is usually seen through the eyes of a single character, typically the one who has the most at stake in the scene.

The scene must have a purpose. Either it advances the plot, or it develops the character, or conveys some important piece of information. In the first few lines, we must set the scene (show where we are in time and space) and establish who is the POV character.

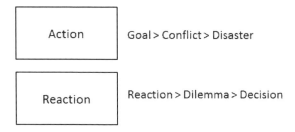

Types of Scene

There are two types of scene, action and reaction. Actions scenes end in a disaster, reaction scenes show the character reacting to what happened and making a decision about what to do next. The two kinds of scenes are arranged back to back, with the action scene getting the reader spun up, and the reaction scene giving them a moment to recover before proceeding on to what's next, usually an even bigger disaster.

Scenes are filled with conflict. There should be as much confrontation or danger as possible within a scene, and the scene should end with a disaster.

Identify Scenes

You've been free writing and have produced the first draft of a story. It has a beginning, middle, and end. You've identified the major turning points, and are ready to think about structural revision.

Break the story into scenes. The scene is the primary unit of storytelling. When you move things around in structural revision, you'll probably want to move whole scenes. Look for parts of the story that occur all in one place, at one time.

Identify the Scene Purpose

All scenes should have a purpose. In revision, ask what purpose a scene serves. If the answer is "none", the scene should be overhauled or cut. Scene purposes include:

Advance the Plot The action in the scene should move the plot forward.

Develop Character The conflicts in the scene, and the way the characters react to them, should be used to reveal who they are.

Convey Information Scenes are allowed to contain info dumps, flashbacks, and character backstory, if that's what necessary to convey information to the reader.

In addition, scenes can be used to:

Create an Emotional Connection with a character, like doing something mean to him to create sympathy.

Foreshadowing Hint at what's coming next. It can be subtle, for example, the use of words with double meanings, a description of a storm brewing, or the last light of day almost gone.

Grease the Skids Show the character using some unusual ability in an ordinary setting, like apparating, traveling back in time, or speaking French. Later, when the character must use that ability in a crisis, the reader has already been groomed to accept that the character can do that.

Builds Suspense A scene holds conflicts, but those conflicts can be intensified with pacing.

Provides Comic Relief to alleviate a dark scene.

Provides a Break Lets the reader recover from the action in the previous scene.

Establishes Mood Scenes can be made rich with description, and description can be a powerful tool for setting mood.

Develop a Theme It's usually a mistake to write a story for the purpose of promoting a theme because the story tends to come across as preachy, but it's a common thing for themes to emerge naturally. When they do appear naturally, it's okay to sharpen them and bring them out more.

Make the Scene More Intense

If the scene doesn't seem intense enough, intensify some of its components. (see pg. 65 for more a more detailed discussion.)

Conflicts Make the obstacles more intimidating, the conflicts scarier.

POV Stay with the same POV throughout, and try using the Deep POV technique used by romance and horror writers to reach the emotions at a visceral way.

Character Development Do something poignant to make the reader feel for your character.

Bait the Hook End the scene with a bigger hook than before. Confront your characters with some problem that seems insolvable, or maybe not even survivable.

Revise Character Development

"A good novel tells us the truth about the hero, but a bad novel tells us the truth about the author."

G.K. Chesterton

Character development is tricky. You can travel faster than light or violate conservation of mass, and the reader will be fine with it, but if your character doesn't seem like a real person to them, or worse, does something a real person wouldn't have done, the reader will put the book down and walk away.

Here are some common problems with character development, with some suggestions for how to fix them.

The Character Isn't Likable

One of the more common problems is a character that isn't likable. If it's your main character that isn't likable, it's a serious problem, but fortunately, one that's easy to fix.

How make a character likeable:

- o Show him doing something most people admire ("Save the cat").
- o Give him good qualities. Make him brave, clever, resourceful, or persistent.
- o Give him an interesting quirk, particularly if it's a weakness or vulnerability ("I hate snakes").
- o Make him suffer an unjust injury.
- o Show him loving someone or something other than himself.
- o Show him having his hopes disappointed.
- o Treat him unfairly.
- o Cast him as the underdog.
- o Make him be funny.

Actually, the character doesn't have to be likable, but he does have to be interesting. This is particularly true for an antihero. Think of Anakin Skywalker when he killed the younglings in the Jedi Temple. He wasn't likable at that moment, but he was definitely interesting.

The Character Has No Flaws

A character with no flaws is called a Mary Sue, a hero too good to be true. The expression comes from a parody of early Star Trek fanfiction,

> *"Mary Sue was the youngest graduate of Star Fleet Academy, only fifteen and a half years old."* [66]

Characters of this type are the youngest, smartest, and most beautiful creatures ever seen in this corner of fandom. They often have striking features, like violet eyes, and an unusual skill, like being a martial arts expert. Mary Sues have no flaws. They're perfect, which makes them not believable and not likeable. Creating a Mary Sue is a common error for a new writer, particularly if they're inserting themselves into the story.

The way to avoid creating a Mary Sue is to give the character flaws. Hermione Granger was the smartest student at Hogwarts, but she was socially awkward, and having no athletic ability at all, she routinely fell off her broom. Indiana Jones was handsome and brave, but he was deathly afraid of snakes.[67] When a character has a flaw, readers like them better.

The Character Doesn't Fix His Flaw

If the hero doesn't face his flaw, or knows about the flaw but doesn't fix it, the story doesn't have a character arc. If you don't have a character arc, you don't have a story.

---

[66] *"A Trekkie's Tale"* by Paula Smith, Menagerie 2, 1973. To be fair, the original Mary Sue was a parody of a well-known fanfiction trope.
[67] Indiana Jones was modeled after archaeologist T.E. Lawrence (Lawrence of Arabia) who was terrified of frogs. "I hate squishy animals."

The Character Is a Stereotype

Especially with minor characters, it's tempting to populate your story with stock characters from central casting, the dumb jock, the pointy haired boss, the moustache-twirling villain. These are fine for the first draft, but in revision, the character should be given more depth.
Look to real people for ideas. The jock may write poetry, the pointy haired boss may coach his kid's T-ball team. Real people are interesting because they can surprise us.

A Real Person Wouldn't Do That

Keep an eye out for everyday examples in your own writing. In one mystery novel, the heroine got up before dawn and looked in the shed, where she discovered a cache of terrorist weapons. She had no reason to go look in the shed, she just did it. (Just as the terrorists had no reason to put weapons in a shed they didn't own.) Real people wouldn't have done that.

Similarly, don't have a character speak in a voice they wouldn't have used. Sometimes the author gives each of the characters the author's own voice, such that common soldiers use the same vocabulary as the ancient scholar.

The Character Is Inconsistent

Granted that storytelling is about growth and change, but your character still has to be consistent.

If the character is an educated person early in the story, he should be so later. If the character is empathetic or kind, those traits should be persistent. Don't lose track of your minor characters and forget what they're like.

We Don't Know the Character

Sometimes a minor character is described in detail, the color of their hair, what they're wearing, the shape of their eyes, yet we come away feeling that we don't know who the character is. We know everything about their surface, and nothing about what lies beneath it.

One author suggests looking at photos while writing about the character, especially ones in which the model is moving. Using verbs instead of adjectives should help.

The Character Is Weak

Some authors define their character by his clashes with the villain. Without adversarial forces, he's just another guy going about his day-to-day life. But if the villain isn't believable, the conflict isn't believable, and the hero's character development falls apart.

The Villain is Two-Dimensional

Villains are not all evil, nobody is. Like a drop of ink in a glass of water, evil goes a long way.

A few years ago, the FBI's Most Wanted list featured a silver-haired man in late middle age, a crime kingpin who was violent and exceedingly dangerous. The profile also said he liked to attend lectures and visit Civil War battlefields. A violent crime lord is ordinary, but a crime lord who was a scholar and intellectual, that was memorable.

Later, the list featured included a psychiatric patient wanted for murder. He was described as intense and self-absorbed. He's also an avid outdoorsman and licensed amateur pilot who learned to fly in Botswana, Africa. Psychotic murderers are cliché, one who's a bush pilot with outdoor survival skills, that could be in a novel.

The Villain's Motive is Unclear

A cardboard cut-out villain who's evil for the sake of being evil isn't interesting. Real people are a mixture of good and bad. The main character must have some negative traits to be likeable, and the villain must have some good traits to be interesting.

The villain will only seem real if he has an understandable motivation. Sometimes the villain is after revenge. Sometimes he's accumulating wealth or power and the hero is in the way. Competition is a plausible motivation. Both the hero and villain want the same thing, but only one can have it, a piece of land, control of the company, world domination. A villain competing with the hero for no reason doesn't make sense. A villain with his own family to feed, just like the hero, does.

Sometimes the worst villain of all is the misguided idealist who thinks he's doing the right thing, but is going about it in the wrong way. Tolkien said of Sauron, *"It had been his virtue that he loved order and coordination, and disliked all confusion and wasteful friction."* [68] Sauron loved Middle Earth, which he expressed by trying to control it.

It's unlikely that someone who becomes radicalized is either a sadist or a psychopath, but because he's fighting for the One True Cause, he might be more dangerous than either of them.

Sometimes the villain isn't a villain at all. He's just minding his own business when the hero decides to go after him.

It took me years to realize that the Nellie Oleson character in Little House on the Prairie hadn't done very much wrong to Laura, she was the villain because Laura didn't like her. Nellie had fussy clothes and hair, which Laura resented. In a typical conflict between the two of them, Laura tricked Nellie into standing in the shallow water where she would get leeches. [69]

Scrivener for Revision

You've just completed the first draft of your manuscript. It's filled with great ideas and tells a wonderful story, but it doesn't have a well-defined structure. What do you do next?

Copy/paste your manuscript into Scrivener. The document will be written to one gigantic index card. The text formatting will look the same, so will any images in the document.

Split off pieces of the card, and give them names. For example, each card could be a scene. Split the card into pieces, and give each piece a name. If those pieces are still too big to manage easily, split them into smaller pieces, and give them names. Your larger groups might be chapters, your smaller cards might be scenes. If you stack the scenes

---

[68] J.R.R.Tolkien, Morgoth's Ring
[69] "On the Banks of Plum Creek" by Laura Ingles Wilder.

under the chapters, you can hide them out of sight when you're not using them.

Free writing generates a lot of ideas, some great, others less great. One of the tasks in revision is to figure out what to cut. In Scrivener, you don't lose the things you cut. A few lines can be put in the marginal notes, and whole cards can be moved to the reference section where they won't be deleted by accident.

I have an easier time cutting something by setting it aside than by deleting it. It's the same principle as the housecleaning practice called Purgatory. If you're trying to decide whether or not to throw out an old toy, put it in Purgatory, a box on top of the refrigerator. If you haven't thought of it after a month, it's safe to throw it out.

In free writing, ideas mature over time. The inn becomes "The Merchant's Last Coin", and the foreign city becomes a mudbrick fortification rising from the shifting sands, silken pennants snapping in the desert wind. The reader expects the full description the first time something's introduced, even though the author tends to think them up further along development of the story.

The split screen lets you can look at widely separated parts of the document at the same time, without scrolling between them. It's also useful if you think you might have repeated yourself. You can compare two passages and assure yourself they're different.

The split screen feature can also be used to insert foreshadowing. Suppose something happens late in the story, and you want to drop hints earlier, which you didn't because when you wrote the early part of the story, it was before you knew the large, important event was going to happen later.

Summary

"This material isn't easy, not like calculus."

A Professor of Statistics

Expertise Slows You Down

K. Anders Ericsson (1991) said that beginners can produce text at the rate of handwriting speed, but experts cannot. Experts work harder in all phases of writing.

Experienced writers take longer than novices to produce pieces of the same length. They plan before they start to write, revise afterwards, and employ the techniques of the craft, Show not Tell, Deep POV, and the construction of fluent wording. As in any trade, skilled craftsmanship takes longer.

Two Measures of Writing Speed - Drafting and Overall

The "Write Fast" books say you can write 2,000 words a day or more. Let's say you've been writing a page a day (250-300 words) over the course of a year, and think you're doing badly. You may not be doing so badly as you think.

Be aware that there are two measures of writing speed, drafting and finished. Drafting is the rate at which you can crank out narrative exposition. In NaNoWriMo, contestants try to do 1667 words a day. Overall writing speed includes the whole process, from research to copyediting. As a skilled writer, you'll only spend about 18% of your time drafting, and the rest on the skills of the craft.

Keystroke logging

Mariëlle Leijten and Luuk Van Waes (2013) studied the difference between text generated and text used during different phases of writing.

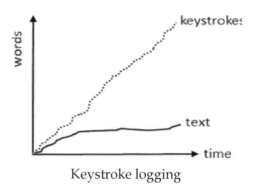

Keystroke logging

Keystroke logging is new, and is becoming an important tool for studying writing processes.

Free Writing

Peter Elbow (1973) found that free writing, or writing a series of drafts without planning beforehand, was one of the best ways to generate new ideas, and the initial spontaneous first draft contained the highest concentration of new ideas.

The Media Affects How You Write

When you write in longhand, you work out what you want to say in your head, and then write things down that are relatively polished. When you type at the computer, your text comes out earlier and rougher. With word processing, everything's easy to fix. When you dictate, there's nothing between you and the words. The sentences come out longer and more complicated, but also and more natural sounding.

You can type faster than you can write in longhand, and you can speak faster than you can type. However the speed at which you can compose new text is less than any of them, so you think it wouldn't matter which media you used. Yet for fast drafting, dictation is two and a half times as fast as either longhand or word processing, possibly because speaking is instinctive and writing is not.

Dictation

Anthony Tovatt (1967) predicted that dictated text would be of higher quality than typed text. The results were inconclusive, but he still believed it to be true.

Ronald Kellogg (1988) discovered that people draft more than twice as fast when dictating than they do when either typing or writing in longhand.

Plan, Draft, Revise - Stages

Gordon Rohman (1964) proposed the first "Plan, Draft, Revise" model. It was a linear model which consisted of three stages, done one after the other.

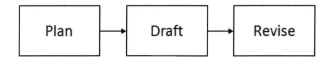

The original PDR model – Gordon Rohman 1964

The Plan, Draft, Revise model was developed to teach novices, who often draft without planning beforehand or revising afterwards, how to write with greater skill. It can also help experienced writers write more efficiently by doing the stages in order.

Plan, Draft, Revise - Problem Solving

Linda Flower and John R. Hayes (1980) published a model of PDR in which planning and revision happened continuously throughout the writing process. This model became the standard as soon as it was published.

Hayes, who studied problem solving and memory, approached writing as a problem-solving task constrained by how much a writer can hold in his head at once. Learning to write wasn't just about learning the different writing processes, it was about learning to juggle them so the writer's cognitive capacity and short term memory weren't overwhelmed.

Flower and Hayes described the difference between novices and expert writers as:

Novices use existing ideas and write them down.

Experts use existing ideas for problem-solving against rhetorical goals, which implies an awareness of the audience, and of what the writer is trying to achieve.

Content Generation

Carl Bereiter and Marlene Scardamalia (1987) expanded on the Flower-Hayes model and described the difference between novice and expert writers as knowledge-telling and knowledge-transforming, in which the higher quality knowledge-transforming text came from the recursive problem-solving process.

Knowledge-telling	Tell what you know
Knowledge-transforming	Reflect on what you know, then make it your own

Knowledge-telling vs. knowledge-transforming

According to them, knowledge transformation is the source of new content, and results in the generation of new ideas.

Outlining

Bereiter and Scardamalia (1987) used the Flower-Hayes model to show why outlining works so well. Generating ideas is a high-level process that uses much of a writer's available thought and memory. The same is true for composing text, the process of turning non-verbal thoughts into words.

If both processes are done at the same time, they compete with each other for resources, and both suffer for it.

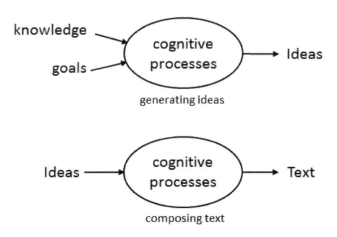

generating ideas

composing text

Outlining separates two high-level processes

Outlining allows you to separate the two processes. Each gets access to more cognitive capacity and more short term memory, so each is done better alone.

A year later, Ron Kellogg (1988) presented convincing evidence that writers working from outlines produce more successful text than writers who draft without planning.

Dual Strategies

David Galbraith (2004) confirmed Kellogg's finding that outlining worked, although Galbraith found it only worked for outliners.

Galbraith noticed an apparent contradiction. Under the Flower-Hayes model, separating idea generation from composing text kept the two processes from interfering with each other and produced better results. Under that model, free writing should produce poor results because it does both processes at the same time.

Yet, Peter Elbow (1973) found that free writing was one of the richest sources of new ideas. In addition, Galbraith found that it seemed to produce more of the high quality text Bereiter and Scardamalia called knowledge-transforming, the thoughtful, reflective prose in which contained the writer's own voice and insights.

Galbraith suggested that two processes were operating in parallel, the familiar outlining process and a second, hidden process, unobserved by either writer or experimenter, which Galbraith speculated had something to do with the way semantic memory[70] is accessed.

Visual vs. Auditory

Most of the planning tools used by Planners are visual aids of one form or another: maps, timelines, drawing, or circle-and-arrow diagrams. Even outlines are as much visual as text-based. And unlike Planners, Pantsers seem to have an easy time expressing their ideas in words, almost as if their thoughts originated in spoken form.

```
Visual → Outliner → Planner

Auditory → Free Writing → Pantser
```

Theory – Planners are Visual, Pantsers are Auditory

I would be willing to believe that Pantsers are mostly visual learners and Pantsers are mostly auditory. I have no evidence to support the theory, but I find it a satisfying explanation.

Don't Try To Change Your Type

There are two widely-recognized writing methods, planner-strategy and revision-strategy, or seat-of-the-pants, in which the writer either plans how to meet the writing goals before starting to write, or adjusts the text to meet the goals after the first draft is generated. According to Mark Torrance (1999), both strategies produce successful text, and both are equally efficient.

---

[70] Semantic memory is a portion of long term memory that has to do with the names of concepts and symbols. It contains general knowledge rather than personal experiences.

Yet seat-of-the-pants writers are often urged to adapt the writing strategies of Planners, even though the quality of their writing is as good as that of Planners. Marleen Kieft (2007) found that, when revision-strategy writers are made to plan beforehand, the quality of their writing declines.

References

*"If I have seen further it is by standing on
ye shoulders of Giants."*

Isaac Newton [71]

In other words,

*"I am never forget the day my first book is published. Every chapter I stole
from somewhere else. Index I copy from old Vladivostok telephone directory."*

Tom Lehrer, "Lobachevsky"

Academic References

Denis Alamargot & Lucile Chanquoy, *"Through the Models of Writing"*,
2001

Veerle Baaijen, David Galbraith, Kees de Glopper, *"Writing: The Process
of Discovery"*, 2010

Anne Becker, *"A Review of Writing Model Research based on Cognitive
Processes"* Ch. 3, Revision – History, Theory, and Practice, 2006

Carl Bereiter, Marlene Scardamalia, and Rosanne Steinbach,
"Teachability of reflective processes in written composition" cognitive
science, pg.173-190, 1984

Carl Bereiter and Marlene Scardamalia, *"The psychology of written
composition"*, 1987

Peter Elbow, *"Writing without Teachers"*, Oxford University Press, 1973

Peter Elbow, *"Writing with Power"*, Oxford University press, 1981

---

[71] Newton was quoting Bernard of Chartres, of 12th century France

References

Peter Elbow, *"Using Careless Speech for Careful, Well Crafted Writing"*, 2013

K. Anders Ericsson, *"Toward a General Theory of Expertise"*, 1991

Linda Flower and John R. Hayes, *"The Cognition of Discovery: Defining a Rhetorical Problem"*, College Composition and Communication, 1980

Linda Flower and John R. Hayes, *"A Cognitive Process Theory of Writing"*, Journal of College Composition and Communication, 1981

Linda Flower, John R. Hayes, L Carey, and Karen Schriver, *"Detection, diagnosis, and the strategies of revision"*, American Psychologist, 1986

David Galbraith, *"Conditions for discovery through writing"*, Instructional Science page 45-72, 1992

David Galbraith and Mark, Torrance *"The writing strategies of graduate research students in the social sciences"*, Higher Education pg. 379-392, 1994

David Galbraith, *"Self-monitoring, discovery through writing, and individual differences in drafting strategy"* Theories, models, and methods in research writing, Amsterdam University Press, 1996

David Galbraith and Gert Rijlaarsdam, *"Effective strategies for the teaching and learning of writing"*, 1999

David Galbraith and Mark Torrence, *"Revision in the context of different drafting strategies"*, Revision: Cognitive and Instructional Processes pg. 63-85, 2004

David Galbraith, *"Writing as Discovery"*, British Journal of Educational Psychology, 2009

John R. Hayes and Linda Flower, *"Writing research and the writer"*, American psychologist, 1986

John R. Hayes and Jane Gradwohl Nash, *"On the nature of planning in writing"*, Chapter 2, The Science of Writing, 1996

John R. Hayes, *"A new model of cognition and affect in writing"* Chapter 1, The Science of Writing, edited by Levy and Ransdell, 1996

John R. Hayes and Ann Chenoweth, *"Working Memory in an Editing Task"*, Journal of Written Communication, 2006

David Kaufer, John R. Hayes, and Linda Flower "Composing Written Sentences", Research in the Teaching of English, page 121-140, 1986

Ronald Kellogg, *"A model of working memory in writing"*, 1988

Ronald Kellogg, *"A model of working memory in writing"* Chapter 3, The Science of Writing, edited by Levy and Ransdell, 1996

Ronald Kellogg, *"Attentional overload: effects of rough draft an outline strategies"* Journal of Experimental Psychology: Learning, memory, and cognition, pg. 355 – 365, 1988

Ronald Kellogg, *"The psychology of writing"*, Oxford University Press, 1994

Marleen Kieft, Gurt Rijlaarsdam, and Hull van den Bergh, *"The effect of adapting a writing course to students' writing strategies"*, British Journal of Educational Psychology, 2007

Marleen Kieft, Gert Rijlaarsdam, David Galbraith, and Hubb van den Bergh, *"The effects of students individual characteristics and writing instruction on learning-to-write"*, British Journal of Educational Psychology, 2007

Marleen Kieft, et al, *"Adapting a writing course to writing strategies"*, pg. 566-578, 2007

Marielle Leijten and Luuk Van Waes, University of Antwerp, *Keystroke Logging in Writing Research: Using Inputlog to Analyze and Visualize Writing Processes.* Written Communication 30(3), pg. 358–392, 2013

Abraham Maslow, "A Theory of Human Motivation", 1943
Gert Rijlaarsdam, Huub Van den Bergh, H. and Michel Couzijn. *"Theories, models and methodology in writing research"*, Amsterdam University Press, 1987

References

Gert Rijlaarsdam and Huub Van den Bergh, *"Writing process research. Many questions, some answers"*, The Science of Writing, 1996

Gordon Rohman and Albert Wlecke, *"Pre-writing, the construction and application of models for concept formation in writing"*, 1964

Mark Snyder and Steve Gangestad, *"On the nature of self-monitoring"*, Journal of Personality and Social Psychology" 51, pg. 125-139, 1986

Mark Torrance, Glyn Thomas, and Elizabeth Robinson, *"The effect of outlining and rough drafting strategies on the quality of short essays"*, paper presented at EARLI SIG writing conference, Utrecht, the Netherlands, 1994

Mark Torrance, Glyn Thomas, and Elizabeth Robinson, *"Individual differences in the writing behaviour of undergraduate student"*, British Journal of Educational Psychology, pg. 189-199, 1999

Mark Torrance, Glyn Thomas, and Elizabeth Robinson, *"Individual differences in undergraduate essay writing strategies"*, Higher Education, pg. 181-200, 2000

Anthony Tovatt and Elbert L Miller, *"The sound of writing"*, 1967

P. Watson, *"Specific thoughts on the writing process"*, in "Cognitive Processes in Writing", page 1129-1139, 1980

Popular References

Plan, Draft, Revise

Jeff Bollow, *"Writing Fast: How to write anything with lightning speed"* (book) Use PDR to write fast.

Rachel Aaron, *"2K to 10K: Writing faster, writing better, and writing more of what you love"* (book) Planning is important, but the top-down revision plan is even more important.

Planning as Sketching

Paul Graham, *"On Sketching"* (blog) Planning in a malleable material.

Fractal Decomposition

Randy Ingermanson, *"The Snowflake Fractal Method"* (blog) Fractal decomposition, "Plan a little, write a little".

Randy Ingermanson, *"Writing Fiction for Dummies"* (book) It describes the snowflake fractal method, and also the three disasters, a simplified version of the Three Act Play.

Randy Ingermanson, *"How to Write a Novel Using the Snowflake Method"* (book)

Story Structure

Larry Brooks, *"Story Engineering"* (book) Story structure for Planners.

Martha Alderson, *"The Plot Whisperer"* (book) Many examples of the Mountain Range diagrams that illustrate plot structure.

Blake Snyder, *"Save The Cat"* (book) Describes beats, the events in a screenplay (and in stories in general).

Jordan E. Rosenfeld, *"Make A Scene"* (book) The definitive book on scene structure.

Janice Hardy, *"What a Concept! Plotting Your Novel Conceptually"* (blog) Sept 2014. Plan how a story unfolds: events that raise the stakes, surprises revealed, what emotions the reader should feel.

Jami Gold, *"The Point of a Scene: Thinking in Concepts"*, Nov 20, 2012.

Daphne Dangerlove, *"How To Write Fan Fiction"* (eBook) 2011. Contains an excellent introduction to constructing a plot using the Three Act Play.

Character Development

Orson Scott Card, *"Characters & Viewpoint"* (book) 1988

Brandilyn Collins, *"Getting Into Character: Seven secrets a novelist can learn from actors"*, (book) 2002

Linda Edelstein, *"Writer's Guide to Character Traits"* (book) 2006

Character Arc

Joseph Campbell, *"The Hero's Journey"* (book) An alternative to the Three Act Play, emphasizing internal turning points, internal changes in response to external events.

Free Writing

Ruth Ann Nordin, *"How To Write By The Seat Of Your Pants"* (blog) May 18, 2013. A romance writer who structures her stories to the conventions of the genre. Advice about what tweaks to make during free writing.

Longhand

Mishka Jenkins, *"Longhand vs. Typing"* (blog) Jan 2014.

Livia Blackburne, *"Typing vs. Longhand: Does it Affect Your Writing"* (blog) Jan 2011. A brain scientist describes how the media affects the writing process.

Carolyn Kaufman, *"Thinking Outside the Computer: Longhand and the Brain"* (blog) Sept 2011. A psychologist and author of "The Midnight Disease: The drive to write" believes she's more creative when writing in longhand.

Dictation

Eric Kent Edstsrom, *"Dictation: I'm a Story Teller, Not a Story Typer"* (blog) February 1, 2012

Revision

Becky Levine, *"Writing and Critique Group Survival Guide"* (book) The source of the checklists for diagnosis

Jami Gold, *"Why Story Structure Matters"* (blog) Jan 2, 2014. On revising structure into the story after free writing. Suggests easy-to-use structures, like Conventions of the Genre and beat sheets.

Jami Gold, *"Can This Story Be Saved?"* (blog) June 4, 2013. Addresses missing turning points, insufficient characters motivation, story pieces don't fit.

Lisa Hall-Wilson, *"5 Substantive Editing Tips For Pantsers"* (blog) 2015. Write a synopsis, reconsider the story length (short story vs. novel) get to know your characters better.

Jefferson Smith, *"Immerse or Die"* (blog) Aug 2014. What takes the reader out of the story? Breaking immersion is as much about story structure and storytelling as it is about poor mechanics.

Leigh Ryan and Lisa Zimmerelli, *"The Bedford Guide for Writing Tutors, fifth edition"* (book) 2010, University of Maryland. Stresses revising from global to mechanics, and offers strategies for writers with visual, auditory, and kinesthetic learning styles.

Perfectionism

Martha Beck, *"Reforming the Perfectionist in You"* (blog) in Oprah Magazine, July 2003. Reject perfection because it will hurt you.

References

About the Author

I'm the daughter of writing researcher John R. Hayes, one the inventors of PDR.

I work as an analyst for a think tank inside the Beltway and live in Northern Virginia with my husband and three children. I'm fascinated by medieval reenactment and write LOTR fanfiction under the name Uvatha the Horseman.

Want to see more? Visit my blog at www.thecraftofwriting.org

Found a typo? Have a story to share about your own writing experiences? Have an opposing view on the lexical and rhetorical strategies used in the generation of successful texts? I'd love to hear from you!

howtowritefaster@gmail.com

Made in the USA
Middletown, DE
09 October 2015